美洲华语课本　第九册

人文　　科学　　历史　　社会　　文学

日常会话　　　常用字词　　　基本句型

目　录

美洲华语课本 第九册
编辑大纲及使用提要

　　「美洲华语」第九册内容的编写是以美洲地区中学九年级学生各项学科的知识水平与生活经验为范畴，从学生的日常家庭生活和学校生活扩展到社会生活以及海外生活圈，大量增加了社会生活实用语言、词汇和文化习俗，因此，「美洲华语」第九册的内容，已经相当于美国高中AP中文上学期课程的程度，本册课文及作业的编写，特别注重辅导学生顺利通过SAT中文测验及AP中文考试。本册作业本还包括33页的SAT阅读练习题，提供学生当暑期作业使用。

「美洲华语」第九册共有六课，每课自成一单元，内容分为以下四大部分：

一、课前活动：引导学生进入教学情境，再开始教学内容，可达到事半功倍的效果。

　　1.让学生借由过去的生活经验或是已学过的知识先进行讨论，帮助学生预先熟悉后面的课文主题。

　　2.每课课前活动的安排是以图片或讨论的方式引导学生了解，并且提供提示，老师带领学生进行讨论，增进学生对新课的学习能力。

二、课文内容：

　　1.「美洲华语」的编写，一向以饶富趣味性和知识性的内容，让学生在有乐趣的情境中学习中文，所以在第九册中，主角程文跟妈妈由美国搬去上海两年。借用程文的经历，扩大读者的生活领域和眼界，同时也大量增加了社会生活实用语言、词汇和文化习俗的知识。在第一课课文〈高兴和难过的眼泪〉中，学习到调职、搬家、转学、申请学校、房屋出租等方面的知识和用语。在第二课课文〈千万别忘了我哨!〉中，学习到旅行、交通、旅馆、高中课程安排等方面的知识和用语。在第三课课文〈亲爱的日记，谢谢你!〉中，学习到有关健康、疾病、医疗、社区义工等方面的知识和用语。在第四课课文〈回台湾过春节〉中，学习到中国菜、小吃和零食、过年的传统习俗、家谱以及台湾历史等方面的知识和用语。在第五课课文〈诗词朗诵比赛〉中，学习看通知、简章、规则以及诗词历史等方面的知识和用语。在第六课课文〈两所大学我都喜欢〉中，学习到有关大学学科、心理、个性、情绪管理等方面的知识和用语。课文的学习策略着重在学生对课文内容（contents）的感受、理解、讨论及发挥。在语言学习方面，尽量运用生活实用语言和词汇，提升语言能力Proficiency level 的层次。课本附录提供问题讨论，老师可以根据问题，引导学生深入探讨课文主题。此外，附录还有课文的英译，帮助学生对课文的理解。

　　2.中国语言（以下称汉语）是声调型语言，发音和语调的准确是学习汉语的基本要求。本书的繁体字版采用注音符号和汉语拼音帮助读者发音。由于少数汉字的发音因地区不同而有别，例如「建筑」的「筑」字，台湾标准发音为二声「ㄓㄨˊ」，中国大陆标准发音为四声「zhù」，本书的作法：注音符号依照台湾标准辞典标注；汉语拼音依照新华辞典，老师采用何种读法请自择。有关儿化韵，汉语拼音加 r，注音符号没法加，所以把字形缩小的

「儿」，附加在字的后面、如「有一点儿」。本册的课文和故事的句子,均以浅蓝色线条标出音步和音步间的停顿如＿＿ ＿＿，在蓝色线中断处才停顿。

三、生字、词语和语文练习：

1. **生字和词语**：在每课课文之后，有一页词语表，列出课文中的生字词和重要的旧字新词，本页有繁简对照及英译。第九册每课生字只有24个，生字以红色字体标出，词语约35-40个，都是日常生活或报章上的常用词语，这些词语中，有一些是"旧"词语，这是根据新、旧混合学习的螺旋式理论，所以，不用把重点放在生字或词语的强记或习写上，而是反复多读课文，熟悉词语的用法。其他课文中比较容易的词语及英译则列在该页课文下面，方便学生查阅。

2. **语文练习**：词语或句型以对话的方式呈现，让学生反复练习并模仿造句。

3. **课堂分组活动**：每课课文之后，有两个至三个分组活动，这些活动是由课文延伸到实际生活中的应用。比如：机场出入境、选课、选择专业、社团活动、看病用语、上餐馆点菜、情绪管理等配合课文之话题。课堂分组活动需由老师引导，学生分组共同讨论并完成。

四、故事阅读及分组活动：

每课课文均附有一个故事，以12至18幅连环图片呈现。生动活泼的连环图画可以吸引学生进入故事的情境引导学生一遍又一遍地读故事、说故事，使学生在故事的情节和对白中，学习如何适当地使用语言。

每课 故事的内容是课文主题的延续、引伸或呼应，并且加深实用语言的运用。比如：第一课故事〈去北京、去上海〉是上海本土的幽默小故事，延续课文中程文搬去上海的话题，内容是提醒学生个性的重要性。第二课故事〈保健气功五禽戏〉是介绍中国武术并让学生演练五禽戏，延续了课文里中文学校上武术课的话题。第三课〈四千里单车行〉是美国高中同学们的友爱故事，呼应了课文里 Relay for Life 的社区公益活动。第四课故事〈友友喝喜酒〉是美国华裔婚礼宴客的小故事，延续课文〈回台湾过春节〉中的传统文化习俗。第五课〈中国的历史朝代故事〉是课文里中国朝代歌的补充，本课故事是以美国九年级学生从 World History 课本中习得的知识为基础，简述中国各朝代重要事件及发明。第六课故事〈林樱的故事〉是引伸课文的主题：情绪、个性和命运，以一个华裔青年（American Born Chinese）奋斗成功的故事，让学生思索品德修养与成功之间的关系，遥遥呼应了第一课故事的内容。

故事中的生字很少，98%以上不是生字，新词在当页附有英译，所以故事的学习策略应着重于对内容的感受和理解，老师可鼓励学生边读边猜，然后分组讨论，试着用自己的语言说出每小段的意思，然后老师再讲解内容，若时间充裕，老师可带领学生逐字逐句念一遍，请多重复生字词，加深学生对生字词的学习。全篇的英译在课本的附录。

美洲华语课本编辑组

2010年10月15日 于美国加州橙县

教学进度设计提要及课程进度表

一、教学进度：

1. 第九册共有六课，教学进度可考虑采用以下的建议：每课进度设为四周：课文上三周，故事上一周。本册第五课故事和第六课故事比较长，老师可定为两周完成。

2. 老师可参照每课课文之后的词语表，所画分的虚线，分成三周学习。词语表之后的语文练习，可让学生以对话式的方式练习效果较佳。

3. 美洲华语是为每周上课二到四小时的中文学校学生而编写的。美洲华语课本每一册的内容，都与该年龄层学生的生活、知识和兴趣相关。若要充分应用「美洲华语」内容，每周上课时数以三小时到四小时最为理想。若每周只上两堂课的班级，可以集中在课文的教学，故事则当成读物使用。

4. 同年级学生的中文程度常常有相当的差距，老师可以配合学生的程度和进步的快慢，随时做适当地调整。例如故事阅读部分，老师可以根据每个学生的语文程度，在 听懂故事内容，到运用自己的语言叙说整个故事，进而自己找资料做更深入的报告之间做调整。

5. 本册丰富有趣的内容不但提高了学生学习的动机，并且为老师在教学上留有弹性的空间。对学生的要求太低或太高都不好，成就感和老师的鼓励，是学生进步的不二法门。

二、作业进度：

1. 每周的作业是配合教学进度而设计的：每课作业分四周（共24页）：课文三周，故事一周。每周作业为六页，星期一到星期四，每天一页，星期五两页。每页可在10-15分钟完成。老师可依学生程度而删增。

2. 本册包括：课本、DVD、字卡及活页的作业本。老师在开学时，可将课本和DVD发给学生，字卡和作业则以逐课和逐周发给学生为宜，以免学生遗失。

3. 为了帮助九年级学生准备SAT中文测验，第九册作业本还包括33页的SAT阅读练习题，提供学生当暑期作业使用。

三、以下是第九册课程进度表及说明，提供给老师们参考使用。

第一、二、三、四课	
第一周	课前活动、第一篇课文、第一周词语、语文练习1、课堂分组活动1
第二周	第一篇课文、第二周词语、语文练习2、课堂分组活动2
第三周	第二篇课文、第三周词语、语文练习3、课堂分组活动3
第四周	复习课文、词语、语文练习、故事阅读、故事分组活动

第五课	
第一周	课前活动、第一篇课文、第一周词语、语文练习1
第二周	第一篇课文、登幽州台、第二周词语、语文练习2、课堂分组活动1
第三周	第一篇课文、今日诗、明日歌、第三周词语、语文练习3、课堂分组活动2

第四周	中国历史朝代歌、 故事阅读、复习课文、词语、语文练习
第五周	故事阅读、故事分组活动、复习课文、词语、语文练习

第六课	
第一周	课前活动、第一篇课文、第一周词语、语文练习1
第二周	第一篇课文、第二周词语、语文练习2、课堂分组活动1
第三周	第二篇课文、第三周词语、语文练习3、课堂分组活动2
第四周	故事阅读、复习课文、词语、语文练习
第五周	故事阅读、故事分组活动、复习课文、词语、语文练习

第一周

一、课前活动：

　　每课的第一页是学生熟悉或见过的图片。老师先带领学生进行课前活动，提起学生对课文的兴趣。

二、念课文：

　　老师解说课文大意并且与学生进行讨论，之后再依照节律符号带领学生朗读，以抑扬顿挫的语调读出课文的情趣。请老师运用「课堂讨论」帮助学生更深一层了解课文涵意，并借由学生的讨论结果了解学生的学习效果。

三、教生字、词语、语文练习

　　学生已念过课文，对生字、生词已不陌生。老师可参照课本分隔成三周的词语画线来区分。学生先透过情境念熟例句，再依例句造出类似的句子。

四、课堂分组活动：这些活动是由课文延伸到实际生活中的应用。由老师引导学生，让各组学生共同讨论并完成。

五、解说作业：

　　学生作业需要老师的解说和指导，请老师在课堂上解说作业内容，甚至指导学生完成一部分，以提高他们回家完成作业的兴趣。

六、上一课的复习测验。

第二周：

一、念课文：

　　老师先复习上周所学的第一篇课文内容，老师引导学生进行讨论，之后再依照节律符号带领学生朗读，以抑扬顿挫的语调读出课文的情趣。

二·教生字、词语、语文练习

　　老师教以分隔线区分的第二周词语，然后再教相关的词语练习。学生先透过情境念熟例句，再依例句造出类似的句子。

三、课堂分组活动

　　老师分组做第二个课堂活动，以相互讨论或访问的方式，让学生练习说话。

四、说明本周作业，可循第一周的模式。

第三周

一、念课文：

　　老师先复习上周所学的第一篇课文内容，然后精读第二篇课文内容，再深入讨论彼此的相关性，参考课本后页的课文提问问题，请学生讨论回答。

二·教生字、词语、语文练习：

　　老师教以分隔线区分的第三周词语，然后再教相关的词语练习。学生先透过情境念熟例句，再依例句造出类似的句子。

三、课堂分组活动

　　老师分组做第三个课堂活动，以相互讨论或访问的方式，让学生练习说话。

四、说明本周作业，可循第一周的模式。

第四周

一、　复习前三周所学的课文、生字和词语。

二、**故事阅读**：

　　故事阅读的重点是在增进学生的理解力和听、说的能力。

1. 老师先用自己的言语把故事说一遍，提起学生的好奇心和求知欲。让学生明白故事中的关键字词。

2. 打开课本，老师可鼓励学生边读边猜，然后分组讨论，试着用自己的语言说出每小段的意思。

3. 然后老师带领学生阅读故事、讲解内容，老师再带领学生逐字逐句念一遍，请多重复生字词，加深学生对生字词的学习。（如果时间不充裕，就不要求学生需逐字逐句地学习。）学生可参看附录中的故事英文翻译。

4. 故事分组讨论，检视学生对故事的了解程度和使用口语回答的能力。

三、说明本周作业：可循前周的模式。

第五周

第五课和第六课的第五周教学内容与第四周同。

第一课 高兴和难过的眼泪

课前活动：你知道上海、北京、西安、台北、香港在哪里吗？
请在下列地图上圈出他们的位置，说说看他们有哪些有名的景点。

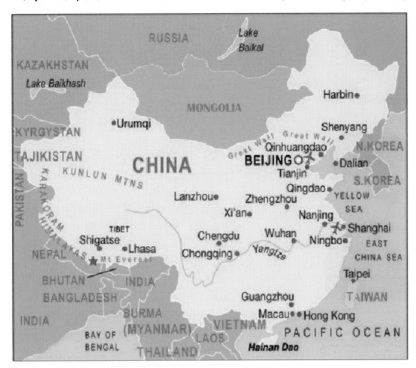

1.

2.

3.

4.

5.

6.

兵马俑（yǒng）、太平山顶、东方明珠、101 大楼、故宫（gōng）、万里长城

第一课　　　课文 高兴和难过的眼泪

（一）　　程文的妈妈在国际建筑公司工作，她是一位资深的建筑师。去年底，总经理想把她调到上海的分公司去工作两年。公司提供的待遇是：

1. 年薪调高三成，外加年终奖金。2. 公司支付程文两年的学杂费用。3. 公司支付公寓和汽车的租金、健康保险和汽车保险。4. 公司支付他们去上海的单程机票（公务舱），并且补助二分之一的行李货运费用（包括空运及海运）。5. 每年可以回美国休假两星期（十个工作天），公司支付来回机票（经济舱）两张。

国际：international　　资深：senior　　总经理：general manager　　分公司：branch office　　待遇：benefits
三成：30%　　年终奖金：annual bonus　　保险：insurance　　行李：luggage　　货运：to ship by freight
空运：to ship by air　　海运：to ship by sea　　休假：to take a vacation　　来回机票：round trip ticket

程文的妈妈认为上海是一个国际化的大都市，充满了朝气，并且是中国经济、贸易和航运的中心，交通四通八达。如果住在上海，她和程文可以常常到中国各地观光，甚至去丝路旅游，深入了解中国的历史、艺术和文化。住上海还有许多其他的好处，例如：1.离台湾近，回台湾看望母亲和公公婆婆都比较方便。2.薪水增加了、开销少了，每个月可以多存一些钱。3.美国的房子可以出租，两年的租金也是一笔不少的收入，这样算来，程文上大学的学费就够了。4.上海有国际学校，学制及课程和美国国内的学校相同，学生随时回美国升学不是问题。

了解：to understand　　公公：father-in-law　　收入：income　　升学：to a higher school

程文的妈妈并没有马上答应总经理的要求，她还得考虑程文的转学问题，也要听听程文的想法。

(二)

程文的妈妈回家以后和程文商量。程文不知道上海是怎样的城市，于是上互联网找

三千道钉纪念碑(上海)

中国馆(2010年世博会)

资料，她在网上看到了上海美丽的市容、繁华的街道、世博会奇特的建筑、东方明珠高塔以及美国赠送的三千道钉纪念碑，表扬勤苦的华工早年对美国的贡献。程文对上海产生了浓厚的兴趣，她和妈妈把搬去上海的优点和缺点列

转学：to transfer school　　商量：to discuss　　互联网：internet　　市容：the appearance of a city
繁华的：prosperous and bustling　　世博会：World Expo　　奇特的：fantastic　　高塔：tall tower
道钉：a spike　　纪念碑：a monument　　贡献：contribution　　产生：to produce; to bring

在一张表上，经过两星期的讨论和思考，她们最后

的选择是搬去上海。

　　一月中，程文从网页上下载了一所国际学校

的入学申请表，她将填好的报名文件，连同

照片、护照影印本和报名费寄去学校，接着，

园林中学把推荐信和程文的成绩单直接寄去

那所国际学校。三月初，学校寄来了通知，告诉

程文她被录取了。

　　程文流下了高兴和

难过的眼泪，她很高兴

去上海，可是她舍不得

离开美国，离开这里

的朋友。

思考 : to think deeply　　申请表 : application form　　文件 : document　　影印本 : photo copy

推荐信 : recommendation letter　　通知 : to notify　　录取 : to enroll; to admit

1.	jiàn zhù 建筑	建築	architectural	21.	pó po 婆婆	婆婆	mother-in-law
2.	jiàn zhù shī 建筑师	建築師	architect	22.	xīn shuǐ 薪水	薪水	salary
3.	diào 调	調	to transfer	23.	kāi xiāo 开销	開銷	expense
4.	tiáo gāo 调高	調高	to be raised	24.	chū zū 出租	出租	for rent
5.	nián xīn 年薪	年薪	annual salary	25.	xué zhì 学制	學制	school system
6.	xué zá fèi yòng 学杂费用	學雜費用	tuition and fees	26.	kǎo lǜ 考虑	考慮	to consider
7.	zhī fù 支付	支付	to pay	27.	biǎo yáng 表扬	表揚	to commend and praise
8.	gōng yù 公寓	公寓	apartment	28.	qín kǔ de 勤苦的	勤苦的	hard working
9.	zū jīn 租金	租金	rent	29.	nóng hòu de 浓厚的	濃厚的	deep
10.	dān chéng 单程	單程	one way	30.	yōu diǎn 优点	優點	merits
11.	gōng wù cāng 公务舱	公務艙	business cabin	31.	quē diǎn 缺点	缺點	demerits
12.	bǔ zhù 补助	補助	to subsidize	32.	liè 列	列	to list
13.	jīng jì cāng 经济舱	經濟艙	economy cabin	33.	xuǎn zé 选择	選擇	to choose, choice
14.	zhāo qì 朝气	朝氣	youthful vigor	34.	wǎng yè 网页	網頁	web page
15.	jīng jì 经济	經濟	economy	35.	xià zǎi 下载	下載	to download
16.	mào yì 贸易	貿易	trading	36.	tián hǎo 填好	填好	to fill out completely
17.	háng yùn 航运	航運	shipping	37.	hù zhào 护照	護照	passport
18.	sì tōng bā dá 四通八达	四通八達	to extend in all directions	38.	chéng jì dān 成绩单	成績單	transcipt
19.	shèn zhì 甚至	甚至	even	39.	yǎn lèi 眼泪	眼淚	tears
20.	yì shù 艺术	藝術	art	40.	shě bù dé 舍不得	捨不得	can't let go

调 (v. to transfer)、　调 (v. to adjust)
diào　　　　　　　　　　*tiáo*

：你知道王主任下个月被调到上海公司当总经理吗？
zhǔ rèn　　　　　*bèi diào*　　　　　　*zǒng jīng lǐ*

：我听说了，他的薪水也调了三倍。
xīn　*tiáo*　*bèi*

补助 (n. allowance)
bǔ zhù

：报纸上说，住家如果改成日光发电，政府会给补助。
zhèng fǔ　　*bǔ zhù*

：听说政府的补助金快用完了，得赶快申请。
zhèng fǔ　*bǔ zhù*

甚至 (conj. even though)
shèn zhì

：小明整天都在玩网上游戏，甚至忘了吃饭睡觉。
zhěng　　*wǎng*　*xì*　*shèn zhì*　　　　　*shuì*

：可不是吗？他的功课一落千丈，甚至有退学的可能。
luò　*zhàng*　*shèn zhì*　*tuì*

一落千丈：to suffer a disastrous decline　　退学：to drop out

这样算来、这样看来、这样说来（这样 +V+来）
zhè yàng suàn lái　*zhè yàng kàn lái*　*zhè yàng shuō lái*　*zhè yàng*　　*lái*

1. 你经常去外州出差，这样说来，你得常住旅馆喽？
zhōu　*chāi*　　　　　　　　　　　　*lǚ*　*lou*

2. 李云工作25年了，这样算来，他可以退休了。
tuì　*xiū*

外州：out of state

考虑 (v. to think over)
kǎo lǜ

：你真的不参加学生会会长的选举了吗？要不要再
xuǎn jǔ

考虑一下？
kǎo lǜ

：我考虑过了，我决定明年再参选。
kǎo lǜ　　　　　　　　　　*cān xuǎn*

参选：to announce candidacy

问题 (n. issue ; question ; problem)
wèn tí

:学生会要举办一场演讲，是关于「升学问题」。

:真好，这是我最关心的问题。谁来演讲？

:王伟民博士。演讲之后，还有提问题的时间。

:太棒了，我正有许多问题要问。他哪一天来？

:十月份吧，等场地问题解决了，我会通知你。

:找场地有问题吗？要不要帮忙？

:不用了，问题不大，不过演讲当天需要你帮忙！

:没问题！我一定到。

表扬 (v. to praise)
biǎo yáng

:大卫的数学每次都考一百分，王老师总是表扬他。

:我认为老师也应该表扬那些有进步的同学。

优点和缺点 (n.strong and weak points)
yōu diǎn hé quē diǎn

:天下没有十全十美的人，每个人都有优点和缺点。

:所以我们不要只看自己的优点，放大别人的缺点。

十全十美 : be perfect in every respect

课堂分组活动一：

根据程文和妈妈的会话，请设计一张房屋出租广告。

:妈妈，我们的房子能租(zū)多少钱？

:这栋(dòng)房子有客厅(tīng)、餐(cān)厅、三间卧(wò)房和两间浴(yù)室，应该(yīng gāi)可以租(zū)个好价(jià)钱。

:我们周围(zhōu wéi)的环境(huán jìng)好、学区(qū)好、交通方便，附近(fù jìn)还有一个公园呢！

:那我们先登(dēng)个广(guǎng)告试试看，每月租(zū)金2500元，不含(hán)水电。

:我们来设计(shè jì)一则(zé)广(guǎng)告，联络(lián luò)电话用家里的吗？

:不，用我的手机号码(hào mǎ)：（350）409-7324。

参考：公寓出租广告

公寓出租
位园林市西南，
近高速公路出口
3房 2.5浴 2车位
交通便利 设有中央冷气
舒适安静 环境佳 近学校
有意者请电 760-279-1529

吉屋出租

课堂分组活动二：

下面是申请美华国际学校需要完成的一些项目，请用中文说说看。

MHIS

Mei Hua International School

Application Checklist

Documents required prior to an admission decision:

1. APPLICATION FORM: This form must be completed, signed and returned to the Office of Admission.

2. APPLICATION FEE: The fee is non-refundable.

3. PASSPORT: Please provide student's passport and 2 photographs of the student.

4. SCHOOL TRANSCRIPTS: Please provide school transcripts of the current school year .

5. SCHOOL RECOMMESATION FORM: This confidential form must be completed by the student's current school.

6. TEACHER RECOMMENDATION FORMS: These confidential forms must be completed by the student's current English and Mathematics teachers.

7. PHYSICAL EXAM FORM: Please provide the student's most recent physical exam within the past three months.

8. STUDENT INFORMATION FORM: This form must be completed and signed by parents.

参考用语：

文件、申请表、签(qiān)字、交回、 报名处、

费(fèi)用、退(tuì)还(hù)、护照、照片、密(mì)件、成绩(jī)单(dān)、

推(tuī)荐(jiàn)表（信）、健(jiàn)康(kāng)检(jiǎn)查(chá)表、资(zī)料(liào)表

课堂分组活动三：

会话情境：王华请他的秘书订一张机票，根据下面的对话和时刻表，你认为王华应该选择哪家公司的班机？请说出三个理由。

王华：星期四下午，我要去旧_{jiù}金山参加一个学术_{shù}会议_{yì}，请你帮我订_{dìng}一张机票_{piào}。

秘_{mì}书：请问你几点钟要报到？什么时候回来？

王华：下午一点半报到，从机场到开会的地点需要半小时的车程。会议在第二天中午结束_{jié shù}，然后我要去中国城逛逛_{guàng guàng}，帮学校买两箱扯铃_{xiāng chě líng}回来。

	西南航空公司	美国航空公司
飞行时段	四小时（转机）	二小时（直飞）
行程	起程：7：30am→11:30am 回程：6：30pm→10:30pm	起程：8：30am→10:30am 回程：5：30pm→7:30pm
票价	$300	$320（经济舱）
行李托运	两件之内免费	每件收$25
机位	没有舱位的分别，登机后自选座位。	设头等舱、公务舱/商务舱、经济舱，需对号入座。
注意事项	至少在起飞前一小时到达机场。 飞机可能误点。	

自从决定（jué bān）搬家以后，程文对上海的人、事、物都感到（gǎn）好奇，有一天，她在网上（wǎng）看到一则（zé）有趣的故事，就讲（jiǎng）给妈妈听。

她说：「有两个乡（xiāng）下人要去城市打工，一个去北京（jīng），一个去上海。他们买好了车票（piào），坐在候车厅（tīng）里等车。他们听见旁边有人在聊（liáo）天，……」

乡下人：villager   打工：to work   候车厅：waiting room

有个人说，我二叔（shū）去上海玩，在上海问路都得给钱。另一个人说，我阿姨（yí）在北京没工作，有个大娘（niáng）又送馒（mán）头又送旧（jiù）衣服，可有人情味了。

带路收费

大娘：aunt (a honorific address for elder woman) 尊称年长的妇人
人情味：human touch

4

那个要去上海的人想，还是北京好，就算找不到工作也饿(è)不死！那个要去北京的人想，还是上海好，连(lián)给人带路都能赚(zhuàn)钱！

带路：to lead the way　　就算：even if

5

于是，这两个乡(xiāng)下人都改变(gǎi biàn)了主意(zhǔ yì)，他们在退票处(tuì piào)相遇(yù)了，原来去北京的人得到了去上海的票，去上海的人得到了去北京的票。

退票处：ticket refund counter

6

去北京的人发现，北京果然好，银行大厅(tīng)里的饮水机(yǐn)可以白喝(hē)，大商场(shāng chǎng)有许多小点心都欢迎(huān yíng)客人试吃(shì)，他没工作竟(jìng)然也没饿(è)着(zháo)。

饮水机：drinking fountain　竟然：actually　白(adv.)：free of charge
白吃、白喝、白用：eat, drink, use without pay

7

去上海的人发现，在上海赚(zhuàn)钱的机会果然多，带路可以赚(zhuàn)钱，看厕(cè)所可以赚(zhuàn)钱，只要多用心、多花力气，就可以赚(zhuàn)钱。他还发现……

果然：really　花（v.）：to spend　力气：strength; effort

8

上海的高楼(lóu)多、绿(lù)地少，于是他就发挥(huī)乡(xiāng)下人的特长，卖起盆(pén)花、盆(pén)土来，一年后，他租(zū)了一个店面(diàn)做生意，收入越来越多，这时他又发现……

发挥：to exploit　　盆花：flower pot　　盆土：potting soil
店面：store

9

高楼的楼面有清洁(jié)公司清洗(xǐ)，但是清洁(jié)公司不洗招(zhāo)牌(pai)，于是他买了人字梯(tī)、水桶(tǒng)和抹(mā)布(bù)，专(zhuān)门擦(cā)招牌，现在他手下有一百多个工人了。

清洁公司：cleaning company　　梯：ladder
他手下：under his leadership　　抹布：rag

10

前不久，他坐火车去北京办事，
刚出车站就遇见一个流浪汉，
两人四目相接，都愣住了，
因为五年前，他们曾经交换过
一次车票。」程文讲完了故事，
她问妈妈的看法。妈妈说：

流浪汉: wanderer　　愣住: to startle　　交换: to exchange

11

「这个故事很精彩！一个人的
个性能改变命运。每个大城市，
比如纽约和芝加哥都有外地
人来打工，有的人很勤劳，
创出了事业，有的人变成了
流浪汉。」

精彩:very interesting　　命运:fate
勤劳:diligent　　创 : to establish; to create　　事业:business

12

程文说：「我明白了，个性真的
很重要。这两个人即使没改变
主意，即使没交换车票，那个
成功的人还是会成功，那个失败
的人还是会失败。」妈妈说：
「我同意你的看法。」

即使:even if　　成功:to success　　失败:to fail

故事课堂分组活动一：

回答下面的问题：
1.本来要到北京的人为什么改变主意到上海去了？
2.本来要到上海的人为什么改变主意到北京去了？
3.到上海的人发现上海有哪些赚钱的机会？
4.说说看这两个人的个性有哪些特点？可参用下面的词语。

参考用语：主动 initiative、被动 bèi dòng、消极 passive、

勤劳 qín láo、用心、进取 jìn qǔ、乐观 guān、灵活 líng quick-witted、努力 nǔ

故事课堂分组活动二：

读一读下面的文章，然后说说看你所知道的上海：

上海市是中国的国际化大都市，上海靠近太平洋海岸，它本来是一个小渔港，1840年鸦片战争以后，由于贸易需要港口，上海才渐渐发展成为大都市。黄埔江是上海的母亲河，黄埔江边的外滩很漂亮，外滩上有许多不同风格的大楼，其中有罗马式、巴洛克式、英国式、法国式、东印度式、中西合璧式等等，外滩是上海最有名的景点之一。

渔港: fishing port [harbour] 贸易:trade 黄埔江:Huang Pu River 滩: beach 风格:style
罗马: Roman 巴洛克: Baroque 中西合璧:Chinese and Western (styles) combined

第二课

第二课 千万别忘了我唷！

课前活动：说说看，旅行要准备哪些东西？

1.

2.

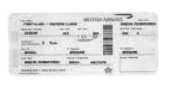
3.

4.

说说看他们在做什么？

5.

6.

7.

8.

9.

10.

行李	登机证 dēng zhèng	护照 hù	机票 piào	检查行李 jiǎn chá	逛免税商店 guàng miǎn shuì shāng diàn
托运行李 tuō yùn	办理登机 bàn lǐ dēng	领取行李 lǐng qǔ		入境检查护照 jìng jiǎn chá hù	

第二课　　课文　千万别忘了我哨！

（一）

亲爱的伙伴们：

经过十四个钟头的长途飞行，我们的班机在昨天下午两点钟到达了上海国际机场，在宽敞的大厅里，我们排队等候入境，轮到我

的时候，我就把护照、登机证和填好的入境登记表，通通交给检查员，他一边翻看护照上的签证，一边客气地问我来中国的目的，我用中文回答他，他亲切地欢迎我来上海读书，并祝我一切顺利！

除了随身带的行李之外，我们还托运了两个又重又大的箱子，入境之后，我们就去行李领取处拿行李，有位同机的旅客帮我们把沉重

钟头：hours　　长途飞行：long distance flight　　班机：a scheduled flight　　到达：to arrive

入境登记表：disembarkation card　　目的：purpose　　行李领取处：luggage claim

的 箱 子 从 行 李 输 送 带 上 拿 下 来，然 后 又 搬 上 推 车，
省 了 我 和 妈 妈 许 多 力 气。玛 丽 阿 姨 带 他 的 儿 子
麦 克 来 接 机，她 说 公 司 在 国 际 大 饭 店 订 了 一 间
套 房，招 待 我 们 住 两 天，然 后 再 搬 到 公 寓 去。
国 际 大 饭 店 很 气 派，它 是 上 海 有 名 的 五 星 级
旅 馆（这 里 的 旅 馆 叫 饭 店 或 酒 店）。我 们 在
柜 台 领 取 了 房 卡，进 房 间 安 顿 好 之 后，就 一 起
出 去 吃 晚 饭。玛 丽 阿 姨 坚 持 请 客，说 是 给 我 们
接 风。

麦 克 是 美 国 学 校 十 年 级 学 生，他 来 上 海 已 经

一 年 了，说 起 中 文 还 是 有 点 儿 洋 腔 洋 调，他 只 学

推车 : a cart　　　接机 : airport pickup　　大饭店 : a hotel　　气派 : style　　　五星级旅馆 : 5 star hotel
柜台 : front desk　　　房卡 : room key　　　接风 : a welcome dinner

会了一句上海话，就是 a la xia xia nong（我谢谢你）。麦克是一个热忱、开朗的男孩儿，他很健谈，我们聊得很开心。亲爱的伙伴们，请常给我发电邮，千万别忘了你们在上海的朋友！

程文上

（二）

亲爱的程文：

那天我和妈妈去机场给你们送行，在高速公路上遇到了大车祸，延误了一小时，等我们赶到机场的时候，你们已经通过安检进入候机室了，没见到你们，真遗憾！

我们已经开学了，Mrs. Lee是我的指导老师，

开学前她约我去谈话，协助我高中四年课程的安排。我说我要多选几门AP课程，如果AP科目考好了，不但大学承认學分，而且比較容易被名校

高速公路：highway　　候机室：departure lounge　　遗憾：a pity　　协助：to assist
安排：arrangement　　学分：academic credit

录取。她问我将来想做什么行业？我说我想要为大众服务，比如当学区教育委员、市议员或市长什么的（哈！哈！）Mrs. Lee 说：「好极了！」她建议我参加学校的辩论社。

这学期我还继续上中文学校，也在准备11月初的SAT中文考试。中文班的许老师说，最近湖人队的 Kobe Bryant 支持洛杉矶的三所中学开武术班，武术老师教学生用中文喊口令，让学生一边练身体，一边练中文，一举两得。所以许老师上中文课时也带我们练五禽戏，让大家用中文喊口令，效果很不错呢。再谈！

明明 上

行业：profession　　大众：general public　　市议员：city counsel member　　市长：mayor

湖人队：the Lakers　　洛杉矶：Los Angeles　　五禽戏：five mimic-animal exercise

	拼音	简体	繁体	英文
1.	huǒ bàn 伙伴	伙伴	pals	
2.	kuān chǎng de 宽敞的	寬敞的	spacious	
3.	dà tīng 大厅	大廳	hall	
4.	rù jìng 入境	入境	to enter a country	
5.	dēng jī zhèng 登机证	登機證	boarding pass	
6.	jiǎn chá yuán 检查员	檢查員	an inspector	
7.	qiān zhèng 签证	簽證	visa	
8.	kè qì 客气	客氣	courteous	
9.	qīn qiè de 亲切地	親切地	friendly	
10.	suí shēn 随身	隨身	take-along	
11.	tuō yùn 托运	托運	to consign	
12.	chén zhòng de 沉重的	沈重的	heavy	
13.	xíng lǐ 行李 shū sòng dài 输送带	行李 輸送帶	luggage conveyor	
14.	dìng 订	訂	to reserve	
15.	tào fáng 套房	套房	a suite	
16.	zhāo dài 招待	招待	to host	
17.	ān dùn 安顿	安頓	to settle	
18.	jiān chí 坚持	堅持	to insist	
19.	yáng qiāng yáng diào 洋腔洋调	洋腔洋調	with foreign accent	
20.	rè chén 热忱	熱忱	zeal	
21.	kāi lǎng 开朗	開朗	open and cheerful	
22.	jiàn tán 健谈	健談	good at conversation	
23.	liáo tiān 聊天	聊天	to chat	
24.	diàn yóu 电邮	電郵	e-mail	
25.	sòng xíng 送行	送行	to see off	
26.	chē huò 车祸	車禍	car accident	
27.	yán wù 延误	延誤	to delay	
28.	ān jiǎn 安检	安檢	security check	
29.	zhǐ dǎo lǎo shī 指导老师	指導老師	advisor	
30.	chéng rèn 承认	承認	to admit	
31.	xué qū 学区	學區	school district	
32.	jiào yù wěi yuán 教育委员	教育委員	school board commissioner	
33.	biàn lùn 辩论	辯論	to debate	
34.	wǔ shù bān 武术班	武術班	martial art class	
35.	hǎn 喊	喊	to yell	
36.	kǒu lìng 口令	口令	command word	
37.	yì jǔ liǎng dé 一举两得	一舉兩得	to kill two birds with one stone	
38.	xiào guǒ 效果	效果	effect	

沉（重）(adj. heavy)；沉重 (adj. serious)

1. 这个箱子很沉，里面全是书。

   书有这么沉吗？我看是金块吧。

2. 他父亲出车祸了，他的心情很沉重。

   他父亲的病情如何？很沉重吗？

安顿 (v. to settle down)

你们已经搬家了吧，都安顿好了吗？

快了，等我们安顿好了，一定请你过来玩。

送行 (v. to see sb. off) 接风 (v. to give a dinner for a sb. from afar)

昨天我们去机场给钱老师送行，怎么没看见你？

我有事不能去，等他明年回来，我们给他接风如何？

好啊，我们请他吃海鲜，多约几个人。

聊 (v. to chat)；聊聊 (v. to have a chat)；聊天 (v. to have a chat)

丽丽，有时间吗？我想跟你聊聊。

好啊！你想聊什么？

也没什么重要的事，就是想找你聊天。

延误 (v. to delay) 延 (v. to extend)

：我们的班机要延后半小时起飞。

：这家公司的票价便宜，但是航班常会延误。

遗憾 (n. regret; pity) (adj. regretful; sorry)

1. ：玛莉说，今晚联欢会有她的歌唱节目，如果不去听会终生遗憾。

：哈哈！她的歌声不怎么样，听了才终生遗憾呢！

2. ：听说学校建游泳池的计画没有被通过。

：那我们的希望又落空了，真遗憾！

承认（肯定、认可）(v. to admit; to accept)

1. ：AP中文考试我得了三分，大学会承认我的高中学分吧？

：很难说！听说要得到四分以上才有希望被承认。

2. ：他承认常玩电脑游戏，但他不承认每天都在玩。

：他明明一放学就玩，他只是不肯承认罢了。

效果 (n. effect)

：听说这种药膏能治好青春痘，效果一级棒。

：我用过这种药膏，效果不大。

药膏：ointment   青春痘：acne

1. 对话练习

白华：我从芝^{zhī}加哥来，坐225号^{hào}班机，请问去哪里领^{líng}李？

服务员：你从国外来，要先通关^{tōng guān}，检查护^{jiǎn chá hù}照，签证^{qiān zhèng}和

入境登^{jìng dēng}记表，然后再去提领^{tí líng}行李。机场的通道

上有指示牌^{zhǐ shì pái}，你不会迷路^{mí lù}的。

白华：谢谢你！225号^{hào}班机的行李在几号转盘^{zhuǎn pán}？

服务员：让^{ràng}我查^{chá}查看……，在六号转盘^{zhuǎn pán}。

白华：谢谢你！

服务员：不客气！

2. 白华到达桃园机场了，请写下入境流程，帮她顺利地离开机场。

| 1. |
| 2. |
| 3. |
| 4. |
| 5. |

31

1. 对话练习

王　英：你好，我叫王英，我已经在网上预订（wǎng yù dìng）了一间单人房（dān）。

服务员：王小姐，您有身份证（fèn zhèng）吗？

王　英：我从美国来的，护照（hù）可以吗？

服务员：没问题！这是您的房卡和早餐券（cān quàn），本酒店提供（jiǔ diàn tí gōng）免费（miǎn fèi）的自助早餐。

王　英：这是非吸烟区（fēi xī yān qū）的房间吧！

服务员：请您放心，本酒店（jiǔ diàn）全面禁烟（jìn yān）。

王　英：太好了！请明天早上七点叫我起床。谢谢！

2. 分组讨论：旅馆提供各式各样的服务，你们能说出几样来吗？

课堂分组活动三：

1. 分组讨论，用中文说说看，以下的高中课程属于哪一类科目？并将其代号填入第二表格中。

高 中 的 课 程 名 称					
1.英国文学	6.交响乐团	11.西班牙文	16.美国政府	21.世界历史	26.合唱团
2.化学	7.木工	12.中文	17.英文写作	22.舞蹈	27.乐队
3.科学	8.美国历史	13.法文	18.戏剧表演	23.英文阅读	28.德文
4.陶艺	9.生物	14.代数	19.地理	24.统计学	29.物理
5.电脑绘图	10.经济学	15.电脑应用	20.微积分学	25.三角学	30.几何学

科目类别	课程名称
外国语言	
语 文	
自然学科	
音乐 艺术	
电脑	
数学	
社会学科	

2. 你们学校有大学先修课吗？有哪些课程？几年级读？

3. SAT考试包括哪三项？总分是多少？

••

陶艺：Ceramics　　生物：Biology　代数：Algebra　　地理：Geography　　统计学：Statistics

物理：Physics　　经济学：Economics　电脑绘图：Computer Graphic　微积分学：Calculus

电脑应用：Computer Applications　　　　三角学：Trigonometry　几何学：Geometry

第二课　　故事阅读：保健气功五禽戏

（请老师在课堂上带领学生做五禽戏，并用中文念口令。全部口令在课本第123-126页。
mzchinese.org连线五禽戏video, 提供老师、学生使用。）

1. 武强是一个有武功的人。他会各种拳术，也会使用武器，他经常担任武打片的武术指导。这学期他答应来中文学校教功夫课，大家都很高兴。

武功：martial or physical arts　　拳术：Chinese boxing

2. 大家在室内运动场欢迎他，武强一上台就说了一个笑话：「有三个会武功的人在喝茶，空中有几只小虫在飞，第一个人拔出日本武士刀在空中挥了两下，一只苍蝇落地了，

苍蝇：a fly

3. 低头一看，苍蝇被切成了三段，第二个人不服气，他拔出西洋剑也挥了两下，一只苍蝇落地了，哇！苍蝇的两排脚不见了。这时，一只蚊子飞了过来，第三个人拿起桌上的牙签，

不服气：not being convinced　　牙签：toothpick

4 晃了两下，蚊子急忙停到玻璃桌面上。仔细一看，哇！蚊子在照镜子，原来它变成了双眼皮。」听到这里，大家都笑坏了！武老师说：「学武术的目的不是

玻璃：glass

5 伤害别人，而是健身和防卫。今天我要教你们"保健气功五禽戏"。五禽戏是模仿老虎、鹿、熊、猿、鸟五种动物的动作，它是两千年前神医华佗

防卫：defense　鹿：deer　熊：bear　猿：ape　模仿：to imitate

6 发明的，现在简化成十个招式，所以很容易学。」武老师又说：「首先，跟我一起用中文念口令，一边念，一边做，才能专心。念会了以后就在心里默念。还有，在练五禽戏的招式之前，

招式：movement

7

先要做起势^{shì}，最后要做收势^{shōu shì}。」武老师说明完了，就开始带大家念起势^{shì}的口令。大家边念边做：「两脚^{jiǎo}分开、与^{yǔ}肩^{jiān}同宽^{kuān}，两眼平视，两膝^{xī}微^{wēi}弯^{wān}，收腹^{fù}，全身放松^{sōng}，

起势：beginning movement　　收势：ending movement
肩：shoulder　膝：knee　腹：abdomen　　放松：to loosen up

8

慢慢吸^{màn}气^{xī}，两臂^{bì}慢慢向前平举^{jǔ}，手掌^{zhǎng}心向下，掌心内转^{zhuǎn}，抱向胸^{xiōng}前，手掌慢慢下按^{àn}到丹^{dān}田，同时吐气。」然后，武老师邀^{yāo}请几位学过武术的同学上台帮忙示^{shì}范^{fàn}。

吸气：to inhale　　吐气：to exhale through mouth　　臂：arm　胸：chest
丹田：the pubic region　　示范：to demonstrate

9

于是 John 和六、七位学过柔^{róu}道、跆拳^{tái quán}道、少林拳^{quán}或太极^{jí}拳的同学上台了，这些同学有点儿基础^{jī chǔ}了，所以学得很快。他们做了老虎扑^{pū}食、小鹿^{lù}奔^{bēn}跑、大熊^{xióng}走路、

基础：base　　扑食：to sprang on　　奔跑：to run in a great hurry

10 猴子摘桃（hóu zhāi táo）、大鸟起飞等动作。大家看得目不转睛（zhuǎn jīng），台上的John，突然双手变成虎爪（shuāng biàn zhǎo），向武老师扑（pū）过去。武老师快速退（sù tuì）了一步，眼看John的脸（liǎn）就要碰（pèng）到地面了，

扑: to throw oneself on

11 武老师把脚轻轻一抬（jiǎo qīng），就把他扶（fú）起来了，大家佩服（pèi）得五体（tǐ）投（tóu）地。武老师笑道：「急不得！练五禽戏（qín xì）的秘诀（mì jué）有三：第一，把自己想成一只勇猛（yǒng měng）的老虎、

佩服: to admire   秘诀: secret (of success); magic code   勇猛的: bold and powerful   五体投地: to admire sb. from the bottom of one's heart

12 安详（xiáng）的鹿（lù）、强壮（qiáng zhuàng）的熊（xióng）、顽皮（wán）的猴子（hóu）和轻灵（qīng líng）的鸟。第二，要用中文念口令。第三，要能坚持（jiān chí），有恒心（héng）。如果能这样做，一定会受益无穷（shòu yì wú qióng）。」

轻灵的: light and bright   顽皮的: naughty   坚持: to stick to
恒心: to persist in   受益无穷: to be benefited inexhaustible

故事问题讨论：

1.学武术的目的是什么？

2.五禽戏是模仿哪五种动物？

3.练五禽戏有哪三个秘诀？

4.五禽戏里你最喜欢哪一个招式？为什么？

故事课堂分组活动：

下面是五禽戏中的几个动作。请模仿图片中的动作，然后说说看，

你是怎么做的？（参考用词：分开、向前伸 shēn、手掌 zhǎng、弯腰 wān yāo、弯膝 wān xī、

抬头、提腿 tuǐ、抬高、挺胸 tǐng xiōng）

 小鹿奔跑 lù bēn	1. 左脚上抬后向前一步，重心在右脚 jiǎo。 2.收腹 fù、背圆 bèi yuán、肩膀 jiān bǎng 向前，两臂前伸 bì shēn 双手变鹿角 shuāng biàn lù jiǎo，手背相对。 3.头在两手臂中间，眼睛往下看，重心向后。
 老虎扑食 pū	
 大鸟起飞	

第三课 亲爱的日记，谢谢你！

课前活动:说说看下列的标示是医院的哪些地方?是做什么的?

1. 急诊 ER

2. 3A加護病房
   3A ICU

3. 收费处

4. 挂号

5. ↖ 41 病房 Ward 41

6. 手　術　室
   Operating Room

7. 儿·科

8. ◄皮膚科

9. 領藥處

10. 护士站

11. ←外科
    骨科
    疼痛科
    運動傷害外科
    心臟外科
    麻醉前訪視

12. ↓8 住院大楼　Inpatient Building
    ↓7 医技大楼　Medicotechnical Building
    ↙6 门诊大楼　Outpatient Building
    ↑3 行政大楼　Adminis ration Building
    ↖1-2 住院副楼　Inpatient Minor Building

（一）

十一月十五日

亲爱（qīn）的日记：

我和妈妈搬（bān）来上海已经三个月了，今天我把

海运寄（jì）过来的书籍（jí）和杂（zá）物

搬（bān）出来整理（zhěng lǐ），看见了爸爸

以前送给我的日记本，这里面

有我九岁（suì）到十一岁的童（tóng）年生活。

在我十岁那年，爸爸经常觉得胃（wèi）不舒（shū）服，

特别是在饭前和饭后，起初（chū）爸爸以为是工作压（yā）力

大，引起消化不良（yǐn xiāo liáng）。后来家庭医生建议他去看

内科医生，检（jiǎn）查的结果竟（jìng）然是肝癌（gān ái），并且已经

到了末（mò）期。外科医生给爸爸开刀，切除（qiē chú）了一部（bù）分

肝脏（gān zàng），手术（shù）还算（suàn）成功。接着，专科医生开始给

爸爸做化学治疗（zhì liáo）和物理治疗，爸爸每天都得吃药、

书籍：books　　杂物：varia　　童年：childhood　　消化不良：indigestion　　建议：to suggest

肝癌：liver cancer　　开刀：surgery　　切除：to cut off　　一部分：partial　　肝脏：liver

专科：specialist　　化学治疗：chemotherapy　　物理治疗：physical therapy

打针、量血压，还常常去验血、验尿、照 X 光。在那段日子里，爸爸非常痛苦，他常常头痛、发烧、呕吐、拉肚子，甚至口腔发炎。爸爸的免疫力很低，每次一打喷嚏，咳嗽或流鼻涕，妈妈就很紧张，如果爸爸伤风或传染上流行性感冒，他的症状就比一般人严重，非得叫救护车送去急诊室不可。爸爸经常住院，医生和护士都说他是最合作的病人，他们说爸爸脾气好，从来不抱怨，也不麻烦别人。眼看着西医治不好爸爸的病，后来他就去看中医、吃中药。拖了一个月，爸爸还是离我们而去。

　　我非常珍惜陪伴在爸爸病床边的那段日子，点点滴滴都写在日记里了，日记分享了我的快乐、悲伤

量血压：to measure blood pressure　验血：blood test　呕吐：to vomit　咳嗽：to cough　流行性：epidemic
住院：to be hospitalized　西医(师)：western medicine doctor　中医(师)：Chinese medicine doctor
中药：Chinese medicine　拖：to drag on　点点滴滴：bit by bit　悲伤：sad; sorrowful

和希望。由于常写日记，我发现我的写作能力、表达能力和思考能力都有进步，我还发现写日记有益于心理健康。亲爱的日记，谢谢你。

(二)

十一月二十三日

亲爱的日记：

今天中中来信说，上个周末他参加了美国癌症协会的接力活动，就是 Relay For Life。以前我每年都参加，我们先向亲友们募款，去年一共募到了 $1200元。活动当天，大家都住帐篷，轮流绕操场走路，二十四小时不间断，表示对克服癌症和预防癌症的行动也永远不间断。我最喜欢晚上的点灯节目，大家心里都有要纪念的人或是要祝福的人，这时可以把他们的名字写在小纸袋

写作：writing　　心理健康：mental health　　美国癌症协会：American Cancer Society

接力：relay　　亲友：family and friends　　轮流：to take turn　　绕：to go circle around

间断：interval　　点灯：light up　　纪念：to commemorate

上，里面点上灯，上千个纸袋围在跑道边，看台上还排了一个大大的HOPE，非常壮观。

在爸爸生病的时候，美国癌症协会的义工们给我们许多帮助、安慰和鼓励。Relay For Life是癌症协会的主要活动之一，每年有几百万人参加，大家同心协力为抗癌、防癌做出贡献。

今天我和麦克聊天，他说上海美国学校也有 Relay For Life，并且像在美国一样，参加的中学生可以得到社区服务的点数，我真高兴在中国依然能继续参加这项活动。

纸袋：paper bag   壮观：spectacular   鼓励：encourage   同心协力：to unite in a concerted effort

点数：service hour

1.	qǐ chū 起初	起初	at the beginning	21.	jí zhěn shì 急诊室	急诊室	emergency room
2.	yā lì 压力	壓力	stress	22.	pí qì 脾气	脾氣	temper
3.	yǐn qǐ 引起	引起	to cause	23.	bào yuàn 抱怨	抱怨	to complain
4.	jiā tíng yī shēng 家庭医生	家庭醫生	family doctor	24.	má fán 麻烦	麻煩	to bother
5.	nèi kē 内科	內科	internal medicine	25.	zhēn xī 珍惜	珍惜	to treasure
6.	jìng rán 竟然	竟然	unexpectedly	26.	yǒu yì 有益	有益	good for
7.	mò qī 末期	末期	last stage	27.	mù kuǎn 募款	募款	fundraising
8.	wài kē 外科	外科	surgery	28.	zhàng péng 帐篷	帳篷	tent
9.	shǒu shù 手术	手術	surgery	29.	cāo chǎng 操场	操場	sports ground
10.	yàn niào 验尿	驗尿	urine test	30.	kè fú 克服	克服	to overcome
11.	tòng kǔ 痛苦	痛苦	suffering	31.	yù fáng 预防	預防	to prevent
12.	kǒu qiāng 口腔	口腔	oral	32.	yì gōng 义工	義工	volunteer
13.	fā yán 发炎	發炎	inflammation; ulcer	33.	ān wèi 安慰	安慰	comfort
14.	miǎn yì lì 免疫力	免疫力	immunity	34.	kàng ái 抗癌	抗癌	anticancer
15.	dǎ pēn tì 打喷嚏	打噴嚏	to sneeze	35.	fáng ái 防癌	防癌	cancer prevention
16.	liú bí tì 流鼻涕	流鼻涕	running nose	36.	gòng xiàn 贡献	貢獻	contribution
17.	chuán rǎn 传染	傳染	contagious	37.	shè qū fú wù 社区服务	社區服務	community service
18.	zhèng zhuàng 症状	症狀	sympton	38.	yī rán 依然	依然	still
19.	yán zhòng 严重	嚴重	serious	39.	zhè xiàng 这项	這項	this (item, work...)
20.	jiù hù chē 救护车	救護車	ambulance				

压力 (n. pressure)

：天天都有考试，我觉得压力好大。

：我把考试当成是一种学习，心情放轻松，压力就小了。

不良 (adj. bad; unhealthy; undesirable; poor)

1. ：交朋友要小心，不要跟不良少年来往。

：是啊，交到坏朋友，会带来不良后果。

2. ：我胃痛，他还劝我喝冰水，真是存心不良。

：你胃痛大概是消化不良，以后要注意饮食。

后果:consequence　　　　存心不良:with evil intent

竟然／居然 (adv. unexpectedly：how could.......)

：他只会打球，功课比我差，竟然／居然被这所大学录取了。

：你竟然／居然不知道，这所大学专门爱录取好球员吗？

专门:specially

非得....不可 (v. have to ...)

：你咳嗽越来越严重了，非得去看医生不可。

：可是今天要考AP化学，我非得去学校不可。

眼看（着） (v. to watch helplessly)

1. 他眼看着自己一天比一天胖，却不肯节食。

2. 眼看着他的病越来越沉重，谁都帮不上忙。

节食: on diet

治病 (v. to treat a disease)；治不好、治得好

: 医生，他的病治得好吗？

: 不是什么大毛病，哪会治不好。

有益于 (adj. be good for)；有利于 (adj. be beneficial to)

1. 多运动有益于／有利于身体健康。

2. 资源回收有益于／有利于环境保护。

资源: natural resources

依然 (adv. still; as before)

: 三年没见了，他依然是那个老样子。

: 我觉得他长高了，只是个性依然没变。

课堂分组活动一：

永健医院门诊表		
11诊 外科 王强 医师	12诊 复健科 黄运明 医师	13诊 内科 唐明云 医师
14诊 骨科 张运 医师	15诊 牙科 李美云 医师	16诊 耳鼻喉科 许钟和 医师
17诊 眼科 石品元 医师	18诊 肠胃科 林美华 医师	19诊 过敏科 杨春英 医师

情境：今天早上，有十四个病人走进永健医院，他们有不同的病症，你建议他们去看哪一科？为什么？

No.	病症	门诊	No.	病症	门诊
1	发烧、喉咙痛		8	腿跌断了	
2	胃痛		9	头痛、流鼻涕	
3	牙痛		10	心脏开刀	
4	皮肤痒		11	呕吐、拉肚子	
5	近视		12	血压高	
6	耳朵发炎		13	糖尿病	
7	消化不良		14	老花眼	

复健:rehabilitation

课堂分组活动二：

请根据下列药单，两人一组，用口语完成医生和病人的对话。

姓　　名:张广原　　　性别:男

药　　名:固立康（降低血糖）

服用方法:每日一次，每次两粒。于饭前30分钟服用。

副作用 ：肠胃不适、头痛、没胃口、体重改变。

注意事项：要用足量开水吞服；服药期间少晒太阳；

　　　　　　不要喝酒；药品过期以后请丢掉。

血糖:blood sugar

病人:医生，我健康检查的结果出来了吗？
<small>jiàn kāng jiǎn chá</small>

医生:你的血糖有点过高，要服用＿＿＿＿＿＿＿＿＿＿ 。

病人:我应该如何服用？

医生:服用方法是 ：＿＿＿＿＿＿＿＿＿＿＿ 。

病人:会有副作用吗？
<small>fù</small>

医生:你可能会＿＿＿＿＿＿＿＿＿，如果很不舒服，要跟我联络。
<small>shū</small> <small>lián luò</small>

病人:我还需要注意些什么吗？
<small>xū</small>

醫　生:有，＿＿＿＿＿＿＿＿＿＿＿＿ 。

课堂分组活动三：

我们参加"Relay for life"活动需要募款，
你有什么好方法吗？

我们办过旧物出售、洗车、卖糖果等等，
效果不错,大家可以试试！

还有什么募款方式可以和队友分享吗？

向父母和亲戚朋友募款，这是一项
有意义的活动，他们会支持的。

假设你们要组队参加六月底周末的"Relay for life"活动。
为了招募队友，需设计一份"动人的"中文电子邮件。
内容要包括：活动目的、活动内容、日期、时间、地点、
招募人数、募款目标等等。在完成以后，请用口语报告。

招募 : to recruit

可上网找更多的资料。http://www.relayforlife.org/relay/

癌症是人类健康的最大敌人，许多人都在为抗癌和防癌而努力。在北加州发生过一个感人的真实故事：几年前，有一个乐观进取、活泼友善的女孩，她叫羊其文。

有一天，她发现腿上有个小硬块，检查的结果是肌肉癌，医生说情形非常不乐观。其文的妈妈非常难过，其文安慰妈妈，她会勇敢地面对。那年她十一年级。

肌肉癌：soft tissue sarcoma　　　面对：to face up

其文开过许多次刀，做过许多期化疗。她经常呕吐、发烧、疼痛，甚至脱发。同学们为她推轮椅，帮忙她做功课；他们还为她折纸鹤，祝她健康长寿。

化疗：chemotherapy　　　脱发：baldness　　　纸鹤：paper crane

4

其文和同学组队参加 Relay for Life，矽谷中文学校的师生也响应了这项活动，大家用行动支持其文克服癌症的决心。其文依然非常用功，高中毕业之后，

响应：to echo　　克服：to overcome

5

其文进入柏克莱大学，她的好友郭絜欣进入波士顿大学。一年后，其文身上的癌细胞已经扩散到肺部和全身了。这时，为了鼓励其文，一向体力不好又不爱运动的絜欣，勇敢地报名

扩散：to spread

6

参加从东岸骑到金门大桥的抗癌活动＊，她想，如果其文看到我能做到，她一定更有勇气抗癌吧！其文感动地哭了，她说，她会去金门大桥迎接絜欣归来。

＊Hopkins 4K for Cancer

<ruby>圣<rt>shèng</rt></ruby><ruby>诞<rt>dàn</rt></ruby>节前，其文住院了，同学们<ruby>赶<rt>gǎn</rt></ruby>回来轮流<ruby>陪伴<rt>péi bàn</rt></ruby>她，大家轻声笑<ruby>语<rt>ràng</rt></ruby>让她快乐。<ruby>絜欣<rt>jié xīn</rt></ruby>问其文：「我还能为你骑车吗？」其文<ruby>含<rt>hán</rt></ruby>笑点点头。几天后，其文去世了，她才十九<ruby>岁<rt>suì</rt></ruby>。

陪伴：to accompany

其文最喜欢<ruby>纸鹤<rt>zhǐ hè</rt></ruby>，在两百多人的<ruby>告别式<rt>shì</rt></ruby>上，同学们用乐<ruby>器<rt>qì</rt></ruby>、歌声、<ruby>鲜<rt>xiān</rt></ruby>花和四百只纸<ruby>鹤<rt>hè</rt></ruby>，向其文告别。他们要把对其文的友爱化为大爱，支持<ruby>抗<rt>kàng</rt></ruby>癌和<ruby>防<rt>fáng</rt></ruby>癌的<ruby>研究<rt>yán jiū</rt></ruby>与活动。

告别式：funeral

<ruby>絜欣<rt>jié xīn</rt></ruby>一边努力<ruby>锻炼<rt>duàn liàn</rt></ruby>身体，一边为四千公里单车行<ruby>募款<rt>mù kuǎn</rt></ruby>，她<ruby>募<rt>mù</rt></ruby>到了美金一万元！这些<ruby>募款<rt>mù kuǎn</rt></ruby>是用来<ruby>盖<rt>gài</rt></ruby>「<ruby>希望<rt>xī wàng</rt></ruby>小<ruby>筑<rt>zhù</rt></ruby>*」的，<ruby>专<rt>zhuān</rt></ruby>门给那些没钱住医院的癌症病人<ruby>居<rt>jū</rt></ruby>住。

锻炼：to exercise　　筑：building　　*希望小筑：Baltimore Hope Lodge

10

暑假到了！5月28日清晨，絜欣、林卓民及队友在Baltimore海边集合，他们把单车的后轮沾上大西洋的水，然后开始了风吹、雨打、日晒、睡帐蓬和睡地板的旅程。

沾：to wet　　旅程：journey

11

他们路过十三州，一路上为癌症中心的病人打气。他们翻过三个大山脉，越过Nevada大沙漠，一路上有惊无险，六十二天之后，终于到达了太平洋岸边的金门大桥。

打气：to cheer up　　山脉：ridge
有惊无险：threatening but not dangerous

12

队友们把单车的前轮放进太平洋，兴奋地欢呼着！这时，絜欣抬头望着蓝天，默默地说：「其文，为了纪念你、为了防癌和抗癌，我做到了，你一定很高兴吧！」

故事分组活动一：

情境：有一天，医生告诉其文，她的白血球数量太低，不能做化疗了，其文很失望。这时候，有一群同学来病房看她，他们走了之后，其文写下了这篇日记。请你读一读并回答以下的问题。

Aug. 15

They were all dressed in red to "represent" my blood cells because red is more festive than white, and it's the good luck color in Chinese culture… Then they started playing piano and singing "If we hold on together" from that dinosaur movie … I started giggling and crying so hard both at the same time, and trying to hug all of them. Even when they left scolding me about sleeping early, I couldn't stop crying.

"If we hold on together, I know our dreams will never die, dreams see us through to forever, as high as souls can fly. The clouds roll by".

Thank you for showing up on my doorstep, thank you for thinking of me, thank you for the hugs … mostly, thank you for pulling me back from the edge of despair and reminding me that wherever I am will never be the end of the world as long as I have friends like you.

I don't know how things are going to turn out tomorrow. But for better or worse, I know that it will always be okay, because I have blessed enough to have you – not only you for, but "all" of you who have been with me through thick and thin and everything in between – in my life.

白血球：white blood cell　　欢乐的：festive　　恐龙：dinosaur
责怪：to scold　　心灵：soul　　边缘：edge　　失望：despair　　幸运的：blessed

问题：

1. 其文无法继续化疗，意味着什么？

2. 同学们为什么都穿红色的上衣？

3. 请把"If we hold on together"这首歌翻译成中文。

4. 请说一说，羊其文心情转变的过程。

♥谢谢羊其文的母亲—周晓宇老师提供的资料。

第四课　回台湾过春节

课前活动：说说看这些干货的中文名称。

1.

2.

3.

4.

5.

6.

7.

8.

xiāng gū	gān bèi	hǎi shēn	ěr	xián	xiāng cháng	chén pí	guì pí	xiā
香菇	干贝	海参	木耳	咸鱼	香肠	陈皮	桂皮	虾米

第四课　课文 回台湾过春节

（一）

　　春节快到了！程文和妈妈飞回台北的爷爷奶奶家过新年。

　　过年前三天，她们跟着奶奶去迪化街办年货，每家店面都堆满了各式各样的干货和应景的甜食，顾客们川流不息，热闹极了。他们买了香菇、干贝、海参、木耳、咸鱼、虾米、香肠等干货和麻油、酱油、陈皮、桂皮、辣椒粉、胡椒粉等调味料，另外，还买了五香瓜子、辣味豆干和芝麻糖等零食，然后兴高采烈地坐计程车回家。

　　一到家就看见爷爷新贴的大红春联，程文看见大门上的福字贴倒了，她很懂事，故意高声说：「福倒了！」，果然，奶奶笑眯眯地

店面 : store front　堆满 : to pile up with　甜食 : sweets　香菇 : mushroom　干贝 : scall　海参 : sea cucumber
木耳 : edible tree fungi　虾米 : dried shrimp　香肠 : sausage　麻油 : sesame oil　桂皮 : cinnamon peel
五香瓜子 : spiced watermelon seeds　辣味豆干 : spicy dried tofu　芝麻 : sesame　笑眯眯 : smiling

接着说：「对！福到了！福到了！」

年三十是除夕（chú xī），叔叔（shū shu）全家从台中赶（gǎn）回来，家里更（gèng）热闹（nào）了。吃年夜（yè）饭之前，大家把糖醋（táng cù）鱼等十道年菜排在祖先（zǔ）牌位（pái）面前，然后由爷爷上香和敬酒（jìng jiǔ），大家跟着恭敬（gōng jìng）地行礼（lǐ）。爷爷说：「祭（jì）祖是中国的传统（chuán tǒng）文化，含有饮水（hán yǐn）思源（sī yuán）的意思。」

全家围炉（wéi lú）吃年夜饭了！除了年菜还有热腾（téng）腾（téng）的火锅。饭后，叔叔、婶婶（shěn shen）和妈妈拿出红包，先孝敬（jìng）爷爷奶奶，然后才给小孩子压岁（yā suì）钱，程文拿到了五份（fèn）红包，一下子变（biàn）成了小富婆（fù pó）。吃完饭，程文跟着大人们一起守岁（shǒu suì），午夜十二点，响（xiǎng）起了鞭炮（biān pào）声，程文高兴地叫道：「新年到了！恭（gōng）喜发财（cái）！」新年早上，孩子们给长辈（bèi）们拜（bài）年，

牌位：ancestor tablets　　上香：to offer incense　　敬酒：to offer wine　　行礼：to bow; to salute
传统：tradition　　围炉：reunion dinner　　热腾腾：steaming hot　　火锅：hot pot　　鞭炮：firecrackers
婶婶：aunt (father's younger brother's wife)　孝敬：to show filial respect for　小富婆：rich little lady

早饭有水饺、年糕和萝卜糕，
表示年年幸运、年年高升的意思。

（二）

大年初二是回娘家的日子。一大早，妈妈和程文带着大包小包的礼物，赶回台南的外婆家。她们一进门就看见满桌子的酒菜，阿姨说，肉燥米粉、砂锅鱼头和盐水鸭，都是外婆亲手做的，程文感受到外婆浓浓的爱。

下午，舅舅的女儿诗美表姐陪程文到处逛逛，台南是文化古都，她们参观了孔庙和安平古堡，古堡前有一座郑成功的石像。表姐

台南孔庙

说：「三百多年前，郑成功带军队攻打台湾，把占领台湾三十八年的荷兰人赶走了，于是福建省和广东省的人民

萝卜糕：daikon cake　　高升：to be promoted to a higher position　　回娘家：back to mom's house

肉燥米粉：rice noodle with minced meat　　砂锅：a clay cooking pot　　亲手：personally

舅舅：mother's brother; uncle　　占领：to occupy　　荷兰：Holland

才大量渡海过来，在这里安居乐业。虽然后来日本占据了台湾五十年，但是数百年来，中华传统文化早已在民间生根了。」

安平古堡郑成功石像

　　程文说：「妈妈说，根据家谱，舅舅是河南陈家的第五十六代子孙，是来台湾的第八代。」

表姐说：「对，爸爸和姑姑的名字是"远"字辈，哥哥、我和堂弟是"诗"字辈，姓名的辈分是按照家谱里的《忠厚传家远、诗书继世长》排的。」

程文说：「我将来也要为子孙编家谱，规定同辈的人，用同一个汉字的拼音当 middle name。」表姐开玩笑说：「别急！别急！今年七夕，奶奶要给你办十六岁的成人礼，你总得先成人，才能结婚吧？」

民间：among the community　　　生根：to take root　　　规定：to stipulate

成人礼：adulthood ceremony

#				#			
1.	bàn nián huò 办年货	辦年貨	to do new year shopping	21.	yā suì qián 压岁钱	壓歲錢	new year gift money
2.	qān huò 干货	乾貨	dry goods	22.	shǒu suì 守岁	守歲	to keep vigil on New Year's Eve
3.	yìng jǐng 应景	應景	appropriate for the occasion	23.	zhǎng bèi 长辈	長輩	elders member of a family ; senior
4.	gù kè 顾客	顧客	customers	24.	bài nián 拜年	拜年	new year's greeting
5.	chuān liú bù xī 川流不息	川流不息	a continuous flow	25.	nián gāo 年糕	年糕	ricecake (for new year occasion)
6.	xián yú 咸鱼	鹹魚	salted fish	26.	yán shuǐ yā 盐水鸭	鹽水鴨	salted duck (a cold dish)
7.	jiàng yóu 酱油	醬油	soy sauce	27.	gǔ bǎo 古堡	古堡	castle
8.	chén pí 陈皮	陳皮	dried orange peel	28.	gōng dǎ 攻打	攻打	to attack
9.	là jiāo fěn 辣椒粉	辣椒粉	hot pepper powder	29.	dù hǎi 渡海	渡海	sail across a sea
10.	hú jiāo fěn 胡椒粉	胡椒粉	black pepper powder	30.	ān jū lè yè 安居乐业	安居樂業	to live and work in peace
11.	tiáo wèi liào 调味料	調味料	spices	31.	zhàn jù 占据	佔據	to occupy
12.	xìng gāo cǎi liè 兴高采烈	興高采烈	in high spirits	32.	gēn jù 根据	根據	according to ; base on
13.	chūn lián 春联	春聯	Spring couplets	33.	jiā pǔ 家谱	家譜	a family tree
14.	chú xī 除夕	除夕	New Year's Eve	34.	zǐ sūn 子孙	子孫	descendants
15.	shū shu 叔叔	叔叔	uncle (father's younger brother)	35.	àn zhào 按照	按照	according to
16.	táng cù yú 糖醋鱼	糖醋魚	sweet and sour fish	36.	zhōng hòu 忠厚	忠厚	honest and toleran
17.	gōng jìng de 恭敬地	恭敬地	respectfully	37.	biān 编	編	to compile
18.	jì zǔ 祭祖	祭祖	make a ritual offering to ancestors	38.	jié hūn 结婚	結婚	to marry
19.	yǐn shuǐ sī yuán 饮水思源	飲水思源	to remember one's root				
20.	nián yè fàn 年夜饭	年夜飯	New Year's Eve dinner				

60

川流不息　(coming and going all the time; come and go in an endless flow)
（chuān liú bù xī）

1. 博物馆正在展览兵马俑，参观的人川流不息。
（bó guǎn　　zhǎn lǎn bīng yǒng）

2. 十号高速公路上的汽车，日夜川流不息。
（hào sù）

兵马俑: terra cotta

兴高采烈　(be in buoyant spirits)
（xìng gāo cǎi liè）

：你看他们兴高采烈的样子，就知道UCLA赢了球赛。
（cǎi liè　　　　　　　　　　　yíng　cài）

：别高兴得太早，下场比赛可能输给我们USC。
（shū）

UCLA: University of California at Los Angeles　　　USC:University of Southern California

含　(v. to contain; to have; to import)
（hán）

：快过年了，我想收集含有十二生肖的成语送给大家。
（jí hán　　　　　　　　xiào）

：这类成语很多，但大部分含意不是很好，比如：胆小
（lèi　　　　　　　　hán　　　　　　　　dǎn）

如鼠、对牛弹琴、马马虎虎等等。
（shǔ　对 tán qín）

饮水思源　(gratitude for the source of benefit)
（yǐn shuǐ sī yuán）

：孙思源，你的名字取得真好。
（yuán）

：这是我爷爷取的，提醒大家要饮水思源。
（tí xǐng　　　　　　yǐn）

yí xià zi
一 下 子 (adv. instantly)

：他太饿了，一下子就把点心吃光了。

ràng
：让他再等一下子，马上就开饭了。

开饭: to serve a meal

ān jū lè yè
安 居 乐 业 (v. to live and work in peace)

yí   xiū dìng
：美国1965年移民法修订以后，华人在这里才开始

安居乐业。

zhàn zhēng   qí shì
：没有战争、没有歧视，这是一个安居乐业的好地方。

修订: to revise   歧视: discrimination

gēn jù   gēn jù
根 据 (according to) ； 根 据 (n. basis)

gēn jù   lì huàn
：根 据 最 新 消 息，丽 丽 换 男 朋 友 了。

suí biàn   gēn jù
：真 的 吗？不 要 随 便 说 没 有 根 据 的 话 唷！

zǒng děi   cái
总 得 ....才 .... (have to...... then)

zǒng děi
：每天总得等你回来了，我才能安心睡觉。

zǒng děi
：我知道，可是我总得把工作做完才能回家。

安心: to feel at ease

课堂分组活动一：

下面是过春节的装饰品和应景的食物，请说一说它们的
名称、内容和象征的意义。

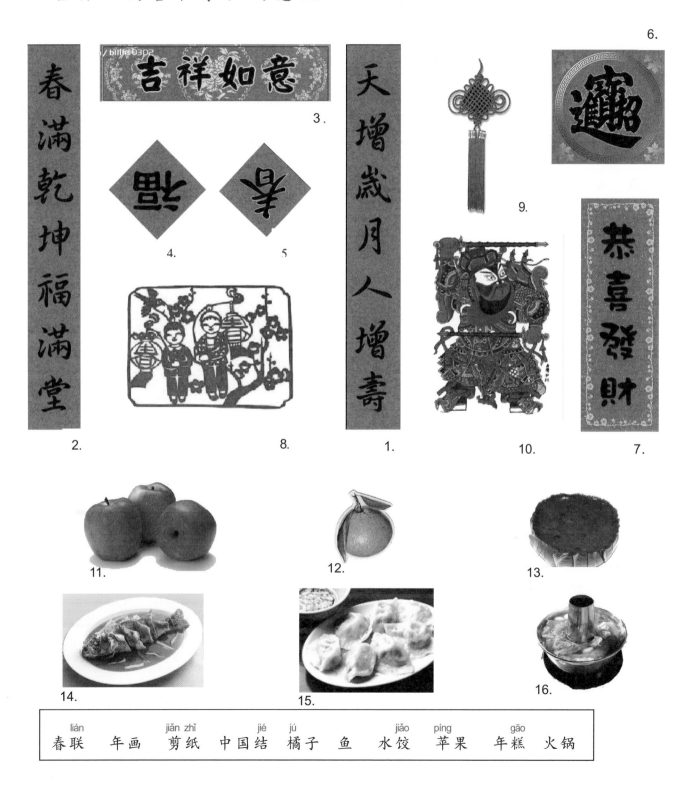

课堂分组活动二：

请参考中华餐馆的菜单，两人一组，完成下面的对话。

价目表

1. 炒时菜 $7.99	6. 宫保鸡丁 $7.99	11. 炸猪排 $7.99
2. 水煮牛肉 $7.99	7. 红烧海参 $7.99	12. 酸辣汤 $7.99
3. 陈皮鸡 $6.99	8. 凉拌黄瓜 $5.99	13. 九香茄子 $6.99
4. 糖醋鱼 $8.99	9. 清蒸干贝 $6.99	14. 蜜汁火腿 $6.99
5. 香菇木耳 $5.99	10. 炒四季豆 $6.99	15. 番茄海带汤 $6.99

A：欢迎光临！请问有几位？

B：我们三个大人，一个小孩。

A：请这边坐。要喝点什么？

B：来壶香片吧！给孩子一杯可乐，我们不要冰水。

A：是。这是菜单，想吃点什么？

B：你能推荐几个菜吗？我们要四菜一汤：一个青菜、一个肉、

两个海鲜，不要鱼。

A：你们看，＿＿＿＿ 、＿＿＿＿ 、 ＿＿＿＿ 、＿＿＿和 ＿＿＿＿ 汤，怎么样？

B：很好，哦！我们还要点外卖，两个素菜，一盒白饭。

A：没问题，我们有 ＿＿＿＿＿ 、 ＿＿＿＿＿ 、 ＿＿＿＿＿ 、＿＿＿＿＿＿ 。

B：好极了，我们就点＿＿＿＿＿和 ＿＿＿＿＿ ，一个辣一个不辣。对了，

请少油、少盐、不要放味精。

A：知道了，请稍坐一会儿，茶和饮料马上就来。

海鲜：seafood　　外卖：food to go　　素：vegetarian　　味精：MSG　　稍：a little while

课堂分组活动三：

A. 读一读

《孔子世家谱》已有两千五百多年的历史，被金氏世界记录列为「全世界最长的家谱」，根据2010年的统计，孔子后裔已经繁衍到第83代《念》字辈了，全世界现在有三百多万人口是孔子的后代。

世家：old and well-known family　金氏世界记录：Guinness World Records　列为(liè)：to enter in a list

统计(yì)：statistics　后裔(yì)：descendant　繁衍(fán yǎn)：to multiply

B. 下面的图表是祖孙三代的称谓(chēng wèi)。你有多少亲戚(qīn qī)？

请按照称谓圈(quān)出来，并说出他们的名字。

亲戚(qī)：relative　称谓：appellation; title

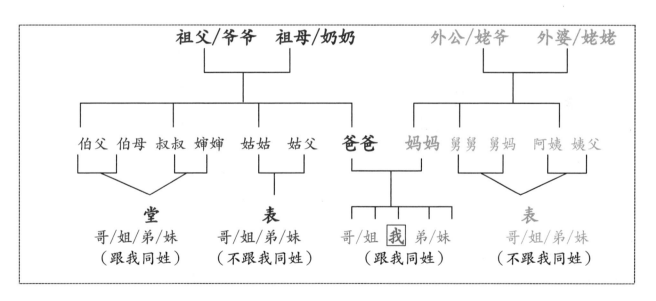

1. 爷爷：_____ 奶奶：_____　外公：_____　外婆：_____

2. 爸爸：_____ 妈妈：_____

3. 我自己：_____，哥/姐/弟/妹：_____

4. 我的**堂**哥/姐/弟/妹 和**表**哥/姐/弟/妹：_____

今天是林友强和黄正香结婚的日子。友强是爷爷的大孙子，是友友的堂哥。今天的婚礼是在一所天主教的教堂举行，晚上在中国城的海鲜大酒店宴请亲友。

天主教：Catholicism　　海鲜：seafood
宴请：inviting to a banquet　　教堂：church

酒店门口的看板上，打出了〈林府、黄府囍宴〉的大红字，客人们欢欢喜喜地盛装出席，有人抱着礼物，有人带来礼金，在签到之后，都交给了收礼的人员。

囍宴：wedding party　　出席：be present
盛装：in beautiful dress　　礼金：cash gift　　签到：to sign in

爷爷、伯父、伯母和新娘的父母是主婚人，他们坐在主桌。友友这桌全是年轻人，友强请服务员特别照顾他们。上菜之前，主婚人致词，说了许多祝福新人的话。

新娘：bride　　照顾：to take care
主婚人：the person who presides over a wedding ceremony
致词：to make an opening speech　　新人：newlywed

66

4

上菜了！服务员说：「一共十道菜，表示十全十美。」她把第一道菜放在转盘(zhuǎn pán)上，又说：「这道拼盘(pīn)里有鸡(jī)、鸭(yā)、鱼、牛肉、海蜇(zhé)皮、海带、香肠(cháng)，很开胃(wèi)的。请慢(màn)用！」

拼盘：assorted cold dishes　　海蜇皮：jellyfish　　海带：kept
开胃：to stimulate one's appetite

5

大家都不好意思先动筷(kuài)子，服务员说：「你们这桌没有主客或(huò)长辈(bèi)，菜在谁的面前，谁就先挟(jiá)吧，然后再顺时针(shùn zhēn zhuǎn)转一圈(quān)，大家轮(lún)流拿好了！」

顺时针：clockwise

6

上过大拼盘(pīn pán)就上汤了，她说：「这是鱼翅(chì)汤，鱼翅(chì)是鲨(shā)鱼的鳍(qí)，又营养(yíng yǎng)又名贵。不过，夏威夷(xià wēi yí)已经不许卖了，以后本地可能也不许卖。来，尝尝(cháng)吧！」于是，……

鱼翅：shark's fin　　鳍：fin　　夏威夷：Hawaii

7

保护鲨鱼成了这桌热门的话题，这时，服务员端来一盘脆皮鸡和一碟椒盐，她说：「这道菜蘸着吃才好吃，请试试看！」于是，大家一边站着吃，一边继续谈论。

脆：crisp　　热门话题：hot topic　　椒盐：spiced salt　　蘸：to dip

8

经理远远看见了，就连忙走过来问：「有什么需要吗？」大家说：「没有啊！」经理说：「请坐，请坐下来吃吧！」大家就坐了下来。过一会儿，服务员来了，她又提醒大家要蘸着吃。

9

友友说：「你说要站着吃，经理说要坐着吃，到底该怎么吃啊？」服务员笑了，她挟起一块鸡，一面蘸椒盐，一面说：「蘸」，友友不好意思地说：「哎呀！我们误会了！」

误会：to misunderstand

10

这时，新郎、新娘过来敬酒了，大家连忙站起来，举起杯子说：「我们以果汁代酒，祝你们幸福快乐。」新郎、新娘说：「谢谢你们的祝福！」

代（替）：to substitute　　新郎：bridegroom　　祝福：blessing

在上了好几道菜之后，服务员捧来一大盘咸鱼火腿炒饭，她说：「上主食了，这是最后一道菜。」又过一会儿，她又端来了水果、蛋糕和汤圆。

主食：staple food

12

她指着红豆汤圆说：「这道甜点是经理送的，祝福新人和大家永远甜甜蜜蜜、圆圆满满。」大家都非常高兴。友友他们也一同举杯，感谢服务员周到的服务。

甜蜜：mellifluous　　圆满：perfect　　甜点：desert　　周到：thoughtful

故事课堂分组活动一：

下面是中餐的餐桌礼仪。说一说，中餐、西餐有何相同的礼仪？有何不同的礼仪？

（一）座位的安排：

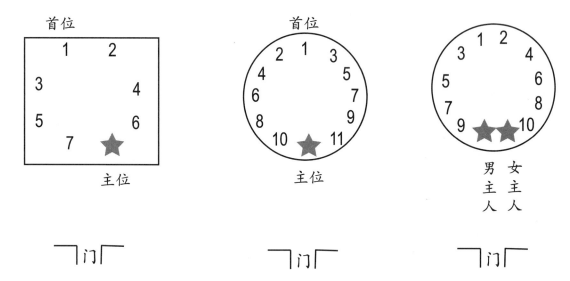

（二）拿碗筷的方法： 不要以口就食，要端起碗吃饭。

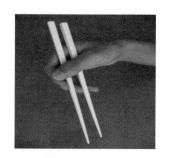

（三）用餐的礼貌：

1. 每道菜皆由主客／长辈开始取菜。

2. 主客／长辈先开动，陪客／晚辈才开动。

3. 如果餐桌上备有公筷，就请用公筷取菜。

4. 从盘中取菜时，不要翻搅。

开动：to start   公筷：common chopsticks   翻搅：to turn around

第五课　诗词朗诵比赛

课前活动：让我们照着下面的规则，来朗诵这两首诗吧！

昨 日 诗 （节录） 佚 名
yì

zuó rì xī zuó rì
昨 日 兮 昨 日 ，

zuó rì hé qí hǎo
昨 日 何 其 好 ！

zuó rì guò qù liǎo
昨 日 过 去 了 ，

jīn rì tú ào nǎo
今 日 徒 懊 恼 。

shì rén dàn zhī huǐ zuó rì
世 人 但 知 悔 昨 日 ，

bù jué jīn rì yòu guò liǎo
不 觉 今 日 又 过 了 ，

bù jué jīn rì yòu guò liǎo
不 觉 今 日 又 过 了 ！

佚名：anonymous　兮：ah　何其：how

徒：in vain　懊恼：annoyed　悔：regret

Yesterday

Beatles in 1965

Yesterday, all my troubles seemed so far away.

Now it looks as though they're here to stay

Oh, I believe in yesterday

Suddenly, I'm not half to man I used to be,

There's a shadow hanging over me.

Oh, yesterday came suddenly.

Why she had to go I don't know she wouldn't say.

I said something wrong, now I long for yesterday.

Yesterday, love was such an easy game to play.

Now I need a place to hide away.

Oh, I believe in yesterday.

Follow the rules below to gain the flawless recitation.

1. No false starts or significant pronunciation errors of any kind.

2. Indicating an excellent grasp of the actual content of the poem and a clear insight into the poet's intention.

3. Whether delivered solely with voice modulations or with other appropriate gestures, reflect a high level of poise and smoothness, free from all visible signs of nervousness.

第五课　　课文　诗词朗诵比赛

（一）

中文学校联合会就要举办春季学术比赛了，比赛的项目包括书法（毛笔组、硬笔组）、中国国画、演讲和诗词朗诵（个人组—限指定诗、团体组—自选诗）。青青他们班上将组队参加诗词朗诵比赛，大家打定主意要拿冠军，志在必得！

许老师问大家要朗诵什么诗，青青说她学过一首唐诗叫《登幽州台》不知是否合适？许老师说：「幽州台是幽州的城楼，幽州就是现在的北京，在唐朝的时候还很荒凉。有一次，

陈子昂随军队来到这里，当时的军旅生活让他感到沮丧、后悔、情绪低落，有一天，他想去幽州台看风景

联合会：association　　春季学术比赛：Spring Academic Competition　　硬笔：pencil; ball pen, etc.
国画：traditional Chinese painting　　组：group　　指定：to assign　　合适：appropriate
随（跟随）：to follow　　军队：troops　　军旅生活：military life　　低落：downcast; be low-spirited

散散心，可是当他登高远望时，反而百感交集，悲从中来，他提笔写下了这首千古佳作。诗中以天、地的久远，衬托出人生的寂寞和短暂；以平淡简洁的语句，说出了人类共同的感伤，所以这首诗特别动人心弦，发人深省，让人思考自我人生的意义和价值。」

　　许老师又说：「你们比赛用这首诗，另外再加上今日诗和明日歌，提醒人们爱惜光阴，这三首诗组合在一起就非常完美了。」中中问：「这两首是新诗和歌曲吗？」

许老师说：「不是，是明朝诗人写的。你们对朝代的先后次序或许没有概念，我来教你们一首朝代歌吧！」

登高 : to climbe　　提笔(拿起笔):to take pen in hand　　千古 : eternal　　久远 : remote　　简洁 : terse

感伤 : sad　　发(启发): to inspire　　省(反省):to examine oneself critically　　意义 : meaning

发人深省 : to make people awaken to the truth　　提醒 : to remind　　或许(也许):perhaps

（二）

登 幽 州 台
dēng yōu zhōu

陈 子 昂 （唐）
chén áng táng

前 不 见 古 人 ，

后 不 见 来 者 ，

念 天 地 之 悠 悠 ，
yōu yōu

独 怅 然 而 涕 下 。
dú chàng tì

今 日 诗   文 嘉 （明）
jiā

今 日 复 今 日 ，今 日 何 其 少 ！
fù

今 日 又 不 为 ，此 事 何 时 了 。
wéi cǐ

人 生 百 年 几 今 日 ，今 日 不 为 真 可 惜 。
wéi xī

若 言 姑 待 明 朝 至 ，明 朝 又 有 明 朝 事 。
ruò gū dài zhāo zhì

为 君 聊 赋 今 日 诗 ，努 力 请 从 今 日 始 。
jūn liáo fù nǔ shǐ

怅然(失意的样子):disappointed; frustrated　　涕(眼泪):tears　　复(又):again　　何其(多么):how
姑待(姑且等待):to merely wait　　朝(日):day　　君(对人的尊称):you
为君(为你):for you　　聊(姑且):merely　　赋(作诗词):to compose (a poem)

明日歌

钱福华（明）

明日复(fù)明日，明日何其多！

我生待(dài)明日，万事成蹉(cuō)跎(tuó)。

世人苦(kǔ)被(bèi)明日累，春去秋来老将(jiāng)至(zhì)。

朝(zhāo)看水东流，暮(mù)看日西坠(zhuì)。

百年明日能几何？请君(jūn)听我明日歌。

中国历史(lì)(shǐ)朝代歌

炎(yán)黄(yáo)尧(shùn)舜夏(xià)商(shāng)周(zhōu)，春秋战(zhàn)国(guó)乱(luàn)悠(yōu)悠(yōu)。

秦(qín)汉(hàn)三国晋(jìn)统(tǒng)一，南朝北朝是对头。

隋(suí)唐(táng)五代又十国，宋(sòng)元明清帝(dì)王休(xiū)。

蹉跎(浪费时间):to waste time　累(拖累):to get sb. into trouble　暮(傍晚): sunset

坠(落下):to fall　炎黄(炎帝、黄帝):Yan and Huang (Yan Emperor and Huang Emperor)

统一:to unite　对头:opponent　帝王:king; emperor　休(休止):to cease; to end

1.	xiàng mù 项目	項目	item
2.	lǎng sòng 朗诵	朗誦	recite
3.	xiàn 限	限	to limit
4.	tuán tǐ 团体	團體	group
5.	guàn jūn 冠军	冠軍	champion
6.	zhì 志	志	will
7.	zhì zài bì dé 志在必得	志在必得	determined to get
8.	fǒu 否	否	no
9.	shì fǒu 是否	是否	whether or not
10.	huāng liáng 荒凉	荒涼	wild
11.	hòu huǐ 后悔	後悔	regret
12.	jǔ sàng 沮丧	沮喪	depressed
13.	qíng xù 情绪	情緒	emotion; mood
14.	sàn sàn xīn 散（散）心	散（散）心	to relax; to ease up
15.	bǎi gǎn jiāo jí 百感交集	百感交集	all sorts of feelings
16.	bēi bēi shāng 悲（悲伤）	悲（悲傷）	sorrow
17.	bēi cóng zhōng lái 悲从中来	悲從中來	overcome by feeling of sorrow
18.	jiā zuò hǎo de zuò pǐn 佳作（好的作品）	佳作（好的作品）	masterpieces
19.	chèn tuō 衬托	襯托	to make more attractive
20.	jì mò 寂寞	寂寞	lonely
21.	duǎn zhàn 短暂	短暫	short
22.	píng dàn 平淡	平淡	flate
23.	xián 弦	弦	string
24.	dòng rén xīn xián 动人心弦	動人心弦	deeply moving
25.	jià zhí 价值	價值	value
26.	ài xī 爱惜	愛惜	to cherish
27.	guāng yīn 光阴	光陰	time
28.	cháo dài 朝代	朝代	dynasty
29.	cì xù 次序	次序	order
30.	gài niàn 概念	概念	idea ;concept
31.	yōu yōu màn cháng 悠悠（漫长）	悠悠（漫長）	very long; endless
32.	ruò 若	若	if
33.	dì wáng 帝王	帝王	king; emperor

限 (n. limit; restrict) (v. to limit)
xiàn

1. 今天中午以前，顺发超级市场有限时大赠送。
shùn chāo jí xiàn zèng

他们只赠送酱油，而且每人限领一瓶。
zèng jiàng yóu xiàn píng

2. 以前这条高速公路限速65哩，现在改成55哩了。
sù xiàn sù lǐ lǐ

是吗？我还没有看见限速标志，请帮我留意一下。
xiàn sù biāo zhì

留意：be careful

指定 (v. to assign)
zhǐ dìng

这次考试李老师指定范围了吗？
fàn wéi

有，除了第二章以外，凡教过的都要考。
chú zhāng

章：chapter

是否 (whether or not)
shì fǒu

你是否还愿意跟他做朋友？
fǒu yuàn yì

那要看他是否跟我道歉。
fǒu qiàn

道歉：to apologize

衬托 chèn tuō (v. to make more attractive)

: 这件礼服很合身，肯定能衬托出你漂亮的身材。

: 颜色也漂亮，把我衬托得更年轻。

身材: figure

概念 gài niàn (n. idea)

: 什么是AP课，我完全没有概念。

: 简单地说，AP课就是大学的先修课程。

自选 zì xuǎn (adj. optional)

: 花式溜冰比赛，包括指定动作和自选动作两种。

: 我比较喜欢自选动作，因为自选动作可以自由发挥。

花式溜冰: figure skating　　发挥: to give free rein to

散（散）心 sàn sàn xīn (v. to relieve boredom)

: 天气真好，不冷不热，很想出去散散心。

: 海边美极了，是散心的好地方。

fǎn ér

反而 (on the contrary)

😀 : 我们送王爷爷闹钟 (nào zhōng) 当生日礼物，他不但不高兴，反而生气了。

😄 : 是啊，我们是好意，没想到反而让王爷爷难过 (nán) 了好几天。

闹钟: alarm clock

ài xī

爱惜 (v. to cherish)

😀 : 有些同学把吃过的口香糖贴 (tiē) 在书桌底下，真是太不爱惜公物了。

😮 : 如果在教室里贴一张「爱惜公物」的标示 (biāo)，也许会有点儿用。

课堂分组活动一：

古时候，中国文人的书房里，必备笔、墨 (mò)、砚 (yàn)、纸四种工具，合称为文房四宝。说说看你的文房四宝是什么？

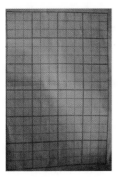

文人: scholar

课堂分组活动二：

A.请读一读这篇书法比赛规则，然后依照下列的评审标准，在下面的格子纸上用铅笔把「登幽州台」抄写一遍，字体大小要均匀，笔法要工整。完成之后，再互相评分。

园林中文学校联合会春季学术比赛

书法比赛注意事项

1.比赛时间为1小时。若迟到15分钟，则不许进场。

2.书法比赛分毛笔组和硬笔组，书写内容将当场公布。

3.毛笔组—请学生自备文房四宝中的毛笔、墨汁（墨）、砚台，大会提供纸张。

4.硬笔组—请学生自备2B铅笔和橡皮擦，大会提供纸张。

5.评审标准：笔画工整：30%　写字笔力：20%　字体大小：20%　整体美感：30%

6.错字、漏字：一字扣一分（同样错误，只扣一次）。

7.请由上至下，右至左书写。

mò
墨汁:ink（墨:ink stick）　砚台:inkstone　橡皮擦:eraser　评审:grading　美感:aesthetic feeling

笔力 : vigour of strokes in calligraphy or drawing　漏字:to skip word　扣 : to deduct　错误:mistake

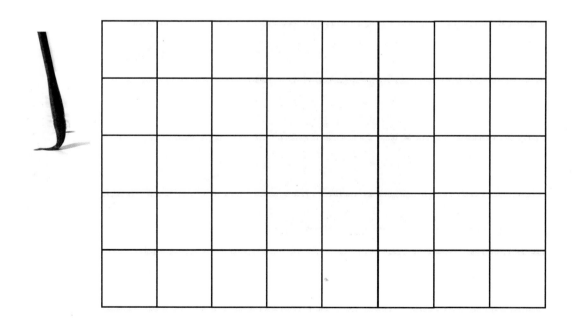

课堂分组活动三：

A. 分组报告：根据下面朗诵比赛的报导，请说说看学生应该注重哪些方面才能胜出？

中文诗词朗诵比赛　追求自然表达

【记者何方方园林市4日报导】

园林市中文学校联合会本年度诗词朗诵比赛于3日在园林高中举行。和往年相比，今年更注重自然地表达情感，减少了「表演」成份。有的孩子发音正确但是动作夸张；有的孩子声音洪亮，但是语调和诗中的意境不合，他们都没能胜出。

---

kuā
夸张：exaggerate　　　shèng
胜出：to win

B. 朗诵练习：请老师指定一至三首诗。各组同学，用正确的发音、自然的语调、朗诵（读）出这首诗的意境。比赛时，其他组的同学当评审，用下面的评分表来评分。

（诗词朗诵评分表）

项目	满分	评　　　　　　　分 （score）				
		第1组	第2组	第3组	第4组	第5组
感情表达 (Express sentiment adequately)	3					
语　调 (Intonation)	3					
发音标准 (Pronunciation)	2					
团队精神 (Cooperate)	2					
总　分 (Total score)	10					
评　语: (Comment)						

1

中国的文化发源于黄河流域。考古学家发现，在七千多年前，中国人已经会做彩色的陶器了。到了四千多年前，炎帝神农氏教人开山种田，之后，黄帝统一了部落，

发源: to originate　流域:river valley　考古学:archaeology

陶器:pottery　部落:tribe

2

嫘祖发明蚕丝、仓颉发明文字，渐渐形成了汉文化。到了公元前两千多年，大禹治水有功，舜把王位给禹，禹传给儿子，建立了中国第一个王朝叫夏，所以中国人或华裔

治水:to prevent floods by water control　传:to pass　王朝:dynasty

3

称自己为炎黄子孙和华夏民族。嫦娥故事里的后羿，还短暂地当过夏朝时期的帝王呢。夏朝之后是商朝，商朝的人发明用牛马拉车，用铜、贝壳当钱做生意，

称自己:call oneself　民族:nationality　短暂:of short duration

帝王:emperor　铜:copper　贝壳:shell　做生意:do business

所以，买、卖、财、货、贵、贱、宝…
这些字里，都有贝字。商朝之后是周
朝，周朝制定了社会阶级制度
和礼节。在公元前770年，周朝分裂
成许多小国家，开始了竞争激烈

制定：to formulate　　阶级：(social) class　　礼节：protocol; etiquette
竞争激烈：keen competition

的春秋战国时期。这个时期产生
了许多思想家、政治家、教育家、
军事家、工程师、文学家，比如：
孔子、老子、孙子、鲁班和屈原。
这个时期的科技也很发达，在
医药、武器、机械、数学、

武器：weapon; military　　工程师：engineer　　机械：machinery

土木建筑、水利工程等方面有
许多发明，包括我们熟悉的九九
乘法表、象棋等等。到了公元前221
年，秦始皇统一全国，并且统一
了文字、货币、车轨、度量衡和

土木建筑：civil construction　　水利工程：irrigation works　　熟悉：familiar
乘法表：multiplication table　　象棋：(Chinese) chess　　货币：money
车轨(路轨)：track　　度量衡：metrology

7

修建万里长城。秦朝(qín cháo)之后是汉朝(hàn)，汉朝扩展(kuò zhǎn)了丝路，增进(zēng)了和西方的往来。楷书(kǎi)成为全国的通用字体。汉朝(hàn)成为一个强大(qiáng)的帝国(dì)，

帝国：empire　　楷书：traditional form　　通用：in common use
扩展：to extend　　增进：to enhance

8

重要发明有：珠算(zhū suàn)、造纸、火药、针灸(zhēn jiǔ)、瓷器(cí qì)、地动仪(yí)等等。
汉朝分裂(liè)后，开始了三国、两晋(jìn)、南北朝时代，经历这三百多年的动乱(luàn)，成就了中华民族(zú)的大融合(róng)。

地动仪：seismograph　珠算：abacus　　火药：gunpowder　针灸：acupuncture
分裂：to disrupt　　动乱：to turmoil　成就：to accomplish
融合：to reconcile mix together

9

民间崇拜(chóng bài)的关公(guān)和发明精确(jīng què)计算圆周率(yuán zhōu lǜ)的祖冲之(zǔ chōng)，都是这个时代的人物。之后，隋朝(suí)统一中国，开通南北大运河、建立(jiàn lì)世界上最早的考试制度(zhì dù)。

崇拜：to worship accurate　　圆周率：pi　　大运河：the Grand Canal

10 　隋朝之后是唐朝，它在文化、经
济、政治、军事、外交、文学、
艺术、科学、诗歌等方面都有伟
大的成就，唐朝使中国的名声远
播。小朋友们熟悉的《静夜思》

外交：diplomacy　伟大：great; mighty　成就：achievement　播：to spread

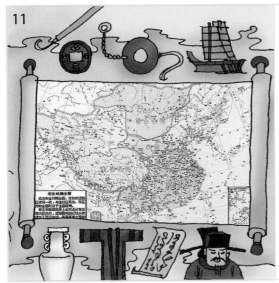

11 　就是唐朝诗人李白写的。唐朝末年
国家分裂成五代十国，中华民族
又经历了一次大融合。接着宋朝
建立了，宋朝的版图小，只好
发展海运和贸易，在农业、科技、
医学、造船等方面求进步，宋朝人

版图：territory　　贸易：trade

12 　把雕版印刷改进成活字印刷、
司南改进成罗盘针、火药做成铁
火炮，发挥了实用功能，影响了
全世界的文明。到了公元1271年，
蒙古人统一中国，建立了元朝，

雕版印刷：to cut blocks for printing　活字印刷：letter press　罗盘：compass
火炮：cannon　　发挥：to give full scope　　蒙古人：Mongolian

成为中国历史上领土最大的朝代。
马可波罗这时来到中国，他的游记引起西方人对中国的向往。
后来，明朝取代了元朝。明朝最伟大的人物是郑和，他带领船队

领土：territory　　马可波罗：Marco Polo　　向往：yearn for
取代：to take over

七次远航，到过马来西亚、印度、波斯和非洲东岸。之后，明朝皇帝烧毁船只，禁止人民航海。这时，欧洲的工业革命促进西方世界现代化。1616年，满族人打败明朝，

远航：oceangoing voyage　马来西亚：Malaysia　波斯：Persia (Iran)
印度：India　烧毁：to burn down　　工业革命：industrial revolution
促进：to boost　现代化：modernization　满族人：the Manchurian

建立了清朝，清朝闭关自守，不注重科技发展，中国很快就落后欧洲了。1840年鸦片战争，中国战败，之后，英国、法国、俄国、日本、德国、葡萄牙，一次次攻打中国，

闭关自守：to close one's doors to the rest of the world　落后：to fall behind
俄国：Russia　　德国：Germany　　葡萄牙：Portugal

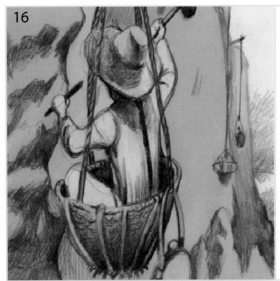

16

占领中国土地、抢走矿产资源和
宝物钱财。短短六十年间，中国
失去1/4国土，人民穷苦，冒险
到海外卖劳力当华工，他们成了
世界各地最早的华人移民。1912年，

占领：to occupy　抢走：to loot　矿产资源：mineral resources
劳力：labour force　冒险：to take a risk　移民：immigrate

17

中华民国成立，推翻了中国数千年
的王朝制度。1937年，日本借故
攻打中国，经过八年战争，1945年
日本投降，并且把台湾岛、澎湖岛
还给中华民国。之后，中国内战，

中华民国：Republic of China　推翻：to overthrow　借故：to find an excuse
投降：to surrender　内战：civil war

18

1949年，中华人民共和国在北京
成立，统治了中国大陆，中华民国
政府迁到台湾。现在，两岸的
人民相互往来，经济、文化、
贸易等关系，越来越密切。

中华人民共和国：the People's Republic of China　统治：to rule
中国大陆：mainland China　迁：to move　两岸：coast to coast　密切：close

故事课堂分组活动一：

口语报告（中文或英文）

你们这一组对中国历史知道多少？请任选一个朝代，分别收集资料，讨论之后，共同做一个五分钟的报告。报告内容需包括：朝代名称、年代、贡献（在政治、经济、文化、科技等方面）、发生的事件和有名的人物介绍，并说明你们的看法和感想。

中国历史朝代表	Dynastic Timetable	
年　代	朝代/时代	Period
2700 BC	炎帝黄帝	Legendary Yellow Emperor
2200 - 1800 BC	夏　朝	Xia Dynasty
1800 - 1100 BC	商　朝	Shang Dynasty
1100 - 256 BC	周　朝	Zhou Dynasty
722 - 481 BC	春秋时代	Spring and Autumn Period
403 - 221 BC	战国时代	Warring States Period
221 - 206 BC	秦　朝	Qin Dynasty
206 BC - 220AD	汉　朝	Han Dynasty
220 - 265	三国时代	Three Kingdoms Period Dynasty
265 - 420	晋　朝	Jin Dynasty
386 - 589	南北朝	Northern and Southern Dynasty
589 - 618	隋　朝	Sui Dynasty
618 - 907	唐　朝	Tang Dynasty
907 - 960	五代十国	Five Dynasty with Ten Kingdoms
960 - 1279	宋　朝	Song Dynasty
1279 - 1368	元　朝	Yuan Dynasty
1368 - 1644	明　朝	Ming Dynasty
1644 - 1911	清　朝	Qing Dynasty
1911 - present	中华民国	Republic of China
1949 - present	中华人民共和国	People's Republic of China

第六课　两所学校我都喜欢

课前活动：说一说你的感觉

1. 轻松

2. 沮丧

3. 焦虑

4. 愤怒

5. 满足

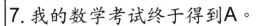

6. 自信

7. 不耐烦

心情报告	号码
1. 又热又渴，却没有水喝！	
2. 刚吃完一顿丰盛的晚饭。	
3. 糟糕！忘了今天要交报告。	
4. 父母希望我的每科成绩都得A。	
5. 大卫跟女生说话常常脸红。	
6. 刚当选为学生会会长。	
7. 我的数学考试终于得到A。	
8. 我已经说了五遍，他还是不懂。	
9. 看到同学被其他同学欺负。	
10. 我只要努力一定会成功。	

8. 害羞

9. 有压力

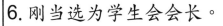

10. 意外

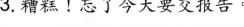
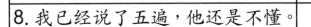
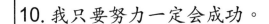
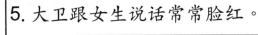

第六课　　课文　两所大学我都喜欢

(一)

明明的姐姐叫晶晶，她是十一年级的学生，暑假过后就要开始申请大学了。晶晶对耶鲁大学和西点军校很感兴趣，于是全家人利用国殇日的三天假期，陪晶晶参观了这两所学校和宿舍，之后又去纽约看望奶奶和姑姑全家。

晚饭后，奶奶和晶晶坐在沙发上聊天，奶奶问她打算念什么专业，晶晶说：

耶鲁大学校园

「还没决定，不过，我对心理、社会、教育这些科系有兴趣。」奶奶说：「这样说来，你的兴趣不是『物』，而是『人』喽！」晶晶说：「是，我对人的『个性和情绪』很感兴趣，比如，个性和遗传的关系；如何管理情绪和控制脾气

耶鲁大学:Yale University　　西点军校:West Point Military Academy　　国殇日:Memorial Day
专业:special field of study　　心理:psychology　　社会(学):sociology　　教育:education
科系:department　　个性:personality　　管理:to manage

等等。」奶奶说：「嗯，这些问题确实(què shí)值(zhí)得研究(yán jiū)，个性和命运(mìng yùn)是分不开的，个性是很多东西的组(zǔ)合，比如：乐观(guān)、悲(bēi)观、内向、外向、自制(zhì)、任(rèn)性、急躁(zào)、冷静(jìng)、贪(tān)心、满足、包容、挑剔(tiāo tī)、活泼(pō)、害羞(hài xiū)…」晶晶说：「奶奶，您在背(bèi)相反词(cí)啊？」奶奶笑道：「别打岔(chà)！你知道吗？一个人若养(ruò yǎng)成自信、善良(shàn liáng)、幽默(yōu mò)的个性，他的生活就快乐得多；一个人若(ruò)常常焦虑(jiāo lǜ)、沮丧(jǔ sàng)、愤怒(fèn nù)、嫉妒(jí dù)、多疑(yí)，那么他的身心就不健康(jiàn kāng)了。」

晶晶说：「这样说来，我们得随(suí)时注意自己的感受，观察(chá)和分析(xī)自己的情绪(xù)变(biàn)化，这样才能有所改进，是吗？」

奶奶说：「对极了，…」

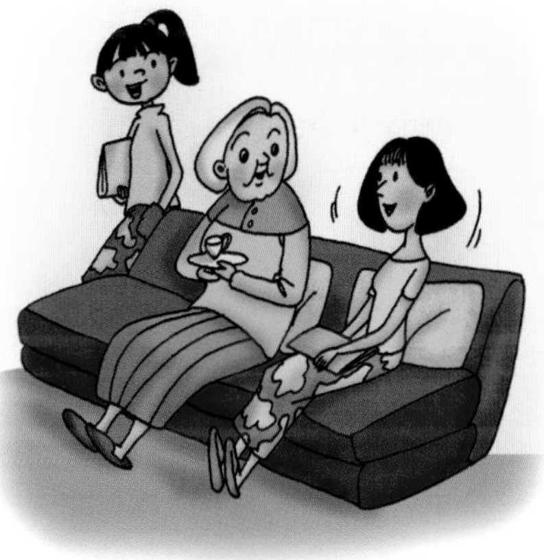

他们聊(liáo)得起劲(jìn)，明明走过来，故意坐在奶奶身旁，

研究：to research　命运：destiny　组合：compose　相反词/反义词：antonyms　沮丧：depressed
别打岔：don't interrupt　感受：deep feeling　变化：change　有所：somewhat　起劲：energetically

她说：「奶奶啊，姐姐最讨厌别人问她升学的事了，她觉得有压力，谁要提起升学的事，她就不耐烦，所以连爸妈都很少问。」晶晶急忙说：「嗳，奶奶当然不一样啦！你别来捣乱！」奶奶笑了！

（二）

奶奶又问晶晶参观学校的感想，晶晶说：

西点军校招生海报

「西点军校的学生充满朝气，西点的教条是：责任、荣誉、意志、勇气、竞争、热忱、服从、尊重、忠诚等等。」

奶奶说：「如果具备这样的品格当然就会成功喽！怪不得报纸上说，连工商界的许多大主管，都是从西点军校毕业的呢！」奶奶又问：「耶鲁大学古典

讨厌：dislike	提起：to mention	压力：pressure	不耐烦：impatient	教条：dogma
具备：to possess	品格：character	怪不得：no wonder	工商界：business circles	
主管：leader				

秀丽，充满了人文气息，你喜欢耶鲁吗？」

晶晶说：「喜欢。耶鲁的校训是"真理和光明"，图书馆前，有一座特别纪念女权的妇女桌，是林樱的作品。在校友名人堂里，陈列了中国第一位

容闳

留学生容闳，以及 Bush, Clinton 等好几位总统的画像。奶奶，我很喜欢这两所学校，但是，要被录取却不容易呢！」奶奶轻松幽默地说：「别担心，尽力去争取。我们晶晶这么

优秀，哪所大学能收到晶晶是他们的福气，否则就是他们的损失了！」

大家听了都笑着说：「晶晶，加油！」

Women's Table

秀丽：beautiful　　人文：humanities　　气息：spirit　　真理：truth　　光明：light　　校友：alumni
陈列：to display　　留学生：foreign student　　轻松：relaxed　　尽力：to try one's best
福气：lucky　　否则：otherwise

1.	sù shè 宿舍	宿舍	dormitory
2.	yí chuán 遗传	遺傳	inheritance
3.	kòng zhì 控制	控制	to control
4.	què shí 确实	確實	indeed
5.	lè guān 乐观	樂觀	optimistic
6.	bēi guān 悲观	悲觀	pessimistic
7.	nèi xiàng 内向	內向	introversion
8.	wài xiàng 外向	外向	extroversion
9.	zì zhì 自制	自制	self-control
10.	rèn xìng 任性	任性	willful
11.	jí zào 急躁	急躁	quick in temper
12.	lěng jìng 冷静	冷靜	calm
13.	tān xīn 贪心	貪心	greedy
14.	mǎn zú 满足	滿足	satisfied
15.	bāo róng 包容	包容	tolérant
16.	tiāo tī 挑剔	挑剔	picky
17.	huó pō 活泼	活潑	lively
18.	hài xiū 害羞	害羞	shy
19.	zì xìn 自信	自信	self-confident
20.	shàn liáng 善良	善良	good and honest
21.	yōu mò 幽默	幽默	humorous
22.	jiāo lǜ 焦虑	焦慮	anxious
23.	fèn nù 愤怒	憤怒	anger
24.	jí dù 嫉妒	嫉妒	jealous
25.	duō yí 多疑	多疑	doubtful suspect
26.	guān chá 观察	觀察	to observe
27.	fèn xī 分析	分析	to analyze
28.	dǎo luàn 捣乱	搗亂	to make trouble
29.	zé rèn 责任	責任	duty
30.	róng yù 荣誉	榮譽	honour
31.	yì zhì 意志	意志	will
32.	yǒng qì 勇气	勇氣	courage
33.	jìng zhēng 竞争	競爭	compete
34.	fú cóng 服从	服從	obey
35.	zūn zhòng 尊重	尊重	respect
36.	zhōng chéng 忠诚	忠誠	loyalty
37.	xiào xùn 校训	校訓	school motto
38.	nǚ quán 女权	女權	woman's rights
39.	yōu xiù 优秀	優秀	outstanding
40.	sǔn shī 损失	損失	loss

观察 guān chá (v. to observe; to inspect)

1. 你知道如何观察(guān chá)自己的情绪(xù)吗？

   就是观察(guān chá)自己高兴、生气、难过(nán)、沮丧(jǔ sòng)的感觉。

2. 我仔细(zǐ xì)观察(guān chá)过河边的露营(lù yíng)地，那里很安全。

   四周(zhōu)的环境(huán jìng)也很重要，应该去观察(guān chá)一下。

有所 yǒu suǒ (to some extent; somewhat)

今天是期末考，大卫居然(mò wèi jū)不来考试。

唉，你有所不知，他昨天突然发高烧，住院了。

起劲 qǐ jìn (adv. with zest and vigor)

爷爷天天玩电脑游戏(nǎo xì)，比年轻(qīng)人还起劲(jìn)。

奶奶要他一起去跳土风舞(wǔ)，他却提不起劲(jìn)。

讨厌 tǎo yàn (v. to dislike)

他吃饭时爱说笑，口水乱喷(luàn pēn)，真令人讨厌(tǎo yàn)。

他说的话也很无趣(wú qù)，我最讨厌(tǎo yàn)跟他同桌吃饭了。

提起 (v. to mention; to speak of)

1. 只要一提起外婆的小白狗，他老人家就很开心。

2. 小白狗把我的帽子咬破了，一提起它我就生气。

不耐烦 (n. impatience)

1. 他常常迟到，我们已经不耐烦听他解释了

2. 每次看牙医都得等很久，真叫人不耐烦。

捣乱 (v. to make trouble)

1. 天气这么热，弟弟还把冷气关掉，真是故意捣乱。

2. 我刚刚在画水彩画，他在旁边捣乱，把水杯也打翻了。

具备 (v. to possess)

：这次钢琴比赛要具备什么条件才能参加？

：至少要六级以上，才有资格报名。

损失 (v. to lose；n. loss)

1. 这场火灾烧掉了两百栋房屋，损失惨重。

2. 他的新车被偷了，又没有保险，损失可大了。

课堂分组活动一：候选人自我介绍

你的社团快要改选干部了，你准备参加竞选，请你根据下面 A,B,C 三项的勾选，做一个简单的自我介绍：

A.
□社长　□副社长
□秘书　□活动
□财务　□公关

> 我的兴趣和我的个性适合哪个职位呢？让我想想看！

> 我在这些方面有什么表现？

B.
__常常照顾社团中的每个人。
__常常自己一个人就能把事情做好。
__喜欢交新朋友，和大家一起说说笑笑。
__喜欢帮助别人解决困难。
__喜欢跟别人讨论各种话题。
__有许多创新的想法，喜欢和大家分享。
__喜欢召集同学一起完成一件事。
__（其他）

> 我有这些能力，让我举例说明。

C.
□口才很好　□表达能力强　□写作能力强
□有团队精神　□有服务热忱　□容易相处
□做事细心　□会电脑设计　□（其他）

课堂分组活动二：学会管理自己的情绪，会让生活变得更美好！读一读下面的小故事，然后依照管理情绪的方法，给美美和小华一些建议：

> 美美和小华约好看电影，电影都上演了小华还没来，美美在电影院门口等小华，用手机也联络不上他，不知发生了什么事。这时，小华跑过来，他笑着正要道歉，没想到美美却冷冷地说：「真是的！怎么又迟到了？」，小华本能地为自己辩护：「路上塞车我有什么办法？」美美生气地说：「每次你都有理由。」小华也提高声音说：「哪里有每次？你不高兴可以先进去看呀！」…本来应该是个快乐的约会，结果…

管理情绪三部曲

第一部：观察自己的情绪：情绪来时，首先深呼吸让自己静一静，然后在想一想：我为何有这种情绪？这种情绪带给我的感觉是什么？

例如：美美因为担心小华发生事情，所以她有_____的感觉，这种感觉使她产生_____情绪。

路上塞车，眼看着要迟到了，小华很_____，这种感觉使他有_____的情绪。

第二部：正确地表达出自己的感受：想一想应该用什么态度与言词来表达自己善意的感觉。

例如：美美如果说：「一直等不到你，不知发生什么事，我_____啊！」

小华听了会说：「_____！让你久等了，_____。」

第三部：抒解情绪有许多方法——往好处想、替对方想、转换注意力、运动、唱歌、找人聊聊、随便写写画画、_____等等。

例如：美美在等候时，可以听听歌，或则_____来抒解焦虑不耐烦的情绪。

小华在被美美埋怨时，她可以_____来抒解不舒服的情绪。

道歉:to apologize　　本能:instinct　　辩护:to defend　　抒解:to relieve　　转换:to change
埋怨:to complain

去年夏天，陈老师带学生去华府旅游，大家坐在草地上午餐，她指着远处说：「你们看！那是林樱设计的越战纪念碑，林樱就是 Maya Ying Lin，她是一位传奇人物。

设计：to design   越战：Vietnam War   纪念碑：Memorial
传奇人物：legendary figure

林樱的父母是从中国来的留学生，后来在 Ohio 大学当教授，1959年，林樱在 Athens 出生了。那时，当地只有他们一家是华人，林樱从小和爸爸、妈妈、哥哥一家四口亲密地生活在一起。

教授：professor   亲密：close

林樱的个性内向，从小爱看书，她是老师的宠儿和同学眼中的小书虫，她喜欢数学和画画，高中毕业后，被耶鲁大学建筑学院录取了，她在那里如鱼得水，非常快乐。

老师的宠儿：teacher's pet   书虫：nerd   建筑学院：architecture college
如鱼得水：to feel just like a fish in water

4

那时，越南战争结束不久，美国损失很大，5.8万名军人阵亡了，35万名受伤，还有许多退伍军人没有工作，社会上充满了矛盾、失望和愤怒的情绪。

结束：to end　损失：to lose　阵亡：to fall in battle　退伍军人：veteran
矛盾：contradiction　愤怒：anger

5

这时，退伍军人提议在华府建一座越战纪念碑，肯定军人对国家的贡献。这件事得到全国人民的响应，1980年，筹办纪念碑的委员会开始向全国征求设计方案。

提议：to propose　华府：Washington D.C　肯定：to affirm　响应：echo
筹办：to make rrangement　委员会：committe　征求：to ask for　方案：project

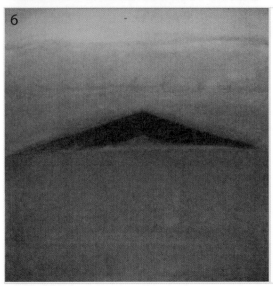

6

林樱很有兴趣。当时传统的纪念碑大多是白色的建筑或雕像，而林樱的设计却是切开地面翻起两页V形黑色光亮的石墙，按照阵亡日期的先后，刻上每位战士的姓名。

雕像：statue　按照：accirding to　刻：to engrave　战士：soldier

7

她的教授鼓励她投稿，在全国1421件匿名方案中，林樱的设计被选中了。这件事轰动全国，但是有许多退伍军人反对林樱的设计，更讨厌她是亚裔。

投稿:to submit for competition　匿名:anonymous　被选中:to be accepted
轰动:to make a stir　讨厌:to dislike; to loathe

8

经过媒体的报导，事情越闹越大，连雷根总统、内政部长、许多有头有脸的国会议员都站在反对的一边。林樱怎么办呢？令人意外的是，21岁的林樱并没有被吓倒，

媒体:mass media　闹:stir up trouble　雷根:Reagan　国会议员:Congressman
内政部长:Secretary of the Interior　有头有脸:having fame and prestige
意外:unexpected　吓倒:frightened

9

她一面勇敢地面对压力和歧视，一面辛苦地争取大家的支持，她打电话给副总统、写信给建筑评论家和上电视节目，说明她设计纪念碑的理念。

歧视:discrimination　评论家:criticism

10

在国会的听证会上，对方要求插国旗和立铜像，林樱坚决反对，最后他们只好把国旗和铜像移开。纪念碑开始建造了，民众能接受这个打破传统的设计吗？大家都在观望。

听证会：hearing　　对方：the opposite side　　要求：to demand
坚决：firmly　　观望：to wait and see

11

批评林樱的声浪还是不断，她很寂寞，于是回到耶鲁念研究所，充实自己。1982年，纪念碑建成了，几万人参加开幕典礼，在开幕典礼上，居然没有人敢提林樱的名字。

批评：to criticize　　声浪：voice　　研究所：graduate school　　充实：to enrich
开幕典礼：opening ceremony　　提：to mention

12

但是，纪念碑却让人们感动得痛哭流涕，人们想起了林樱的话：『当人们读到或是用手触摸到墙上亲人和战友的名字时，心中的悲痛会爆发出来。人们只有面对悲痛、……

痛哭流涕：to cry and shed bitter tears　　触摸：to touch
爆发：to break break out　　悲痛：grieved; painfully sad

才能走出悲痛，开始新的生活。这是建造纪念碑的原意。』纪念碑建成之后，每年有几百万人来这里参观，人们叫它 Healing Wall，它是美国最受欢迎的十大建筑之一。」

原意：original intention

The Civil Rights Memorial in Montgomery, Alabama (1989)

晶晶问：「那林樱后来呢？」陈老师说：「她的才华受到了肯定，她又创作了许多有名的作品。现在林樱是国际知名的建筑师和艺术家，美国民众以她为荣，记者也经常访问她。

才华：brilliant talent　　创作：to create　　国际：international
知名：well-known　　以她为荣：to be proud of her

In 2009, Maya Lin was awarded the National Medal of Arts by President Barack Obama.

林樱虽然是知名人物了，但是她的为人处事依然谦虚、温和、实在。她说她的人生观受到家庭教育和中华文化的影响。她的创作包含了东方和西方的文化。

为人：cultivation of one's mind　　处事：dealing with affairs　　谦虚：modest
实在：down-to-earth　　人生观：philosophy of living　　包含：to contain
家庭教育：family education

MOCA : Museum of Chinese in America
215 Centre St, New York
(212) 334-1057 www.mocanyc.org/visit/

她让两个女儿学中文，她希望他们学习中华文化。为了保存美国的华人移民史料，林樱为纽约市设计的美国华人博物馆（MOCA），已经在2009年落成了。

包含：to contain　保存：to preserve　史料：historical materials
落成：to be completed　MOCA: museum of Chinese American

波田，Storm King Art Center in Mountainville, NY, 2009.

林樱的作品充满了天人合一的理念，现在她更专心于保护自然环境的创作。」陈老师说完林樱的故事，大家便去参观越战纪念碑。晶晶从光亮的墙上看见了自己，……

天人合一：theory that man is an integral part of nature
专心于：to concentrate one's attention on

看见满墙名字浮在人群、树木和蓝天白云之间。前方有华盛顿纪念碑*、后方有林肯纪念堂**，晶晶觉得它们好像在守护着阵亡者，同时提醒人们：国家、荣誉和责任。

多美妙的设计啊！林樱真是个天才！

浮：to float　*Washington Monument　**Lincoln Memorial　美妙：splendid

故事课堂练习：

有一天，晶晶把林樱的故事讲给奶奶听，下面是他们的对话，读一读再回答问题：

奶奶：林樱为什么把越战纪念碑建在地面下呢？

晶晶：林樱说，她要提醒人们，战争之后，留下来的是"伤痕"。

奶奶：我明白了，越战纪念碑远看真像是一道伤痕呢！

晶晶：林樱年轻的时候，承受那么多压力和不公平，她一定很难过！

奶奶：那段时候她一定很辛苦，不过她坚持过来了，真不容易！

晶晶：我想她对自己很有信心，小时候也不怕同学笑她是书虫。

奶奶：读书有许多乐趣，所以不在乎别人笑不笑吧！你怕吗？

晶晶：小时候很怕，现在没人笑了，大家都很用功，因为成绩不好更痛苦。

奶奶：就是！现在知道用功还来得及！

伤痕:scar 承受:to bear 不在乎:not care a bit 不管:no matter

问题讨论：

1.请你说说看，现代战争会怎样破坏地球？

2.你遇到过不公平待遇吗？你是怎么处理你的情绪？

第九册课文课堂问题讨论

第一课

1.公司提出什么条件要程文妈妈调去上海？

2.程文的妈妈觉得搬去上海，对程文有什么好处？

3.请上网查查察看，三千道钉纪念碑的意义是什么

http://www.panoramio.com/photo/2437605 Chinese Railroad Workers Memorial in Shanghai, China. Presented by the State of Illinois. United States of America. James R. Thompson. Governor Gloria Connan. Sculptress January 6, 1991

4.如果由于父母工作的变动，你可能要搬到上海去，请列出优点和缺点。

第二课

1.入境时，海关要检查哪些东西？

2.谁是麦克？他是怎样的一个人？

3.明明去机场为什么没有见到程文？

4. Mrs.Lee 说选 AP 课的好处是什么？

5.今年你在学校修什么课？哪些是必修课？哪些是选修课？

第三课

1.为什么程文的爸爸打喷嚏，她妈妈就会紧张？

2.癌症病人最辛苦的是什么？

3.为什么写日记有益于心理健康？

4.上网查查看 Relay For Life 的活动内容及参加方法。

http://www.relayforlife.org/relay/

5. 你在学校有参加哪些社团?参加哪些社区服务？

第四课

1.过年要吃什么特别的东西？你知道它们有什么特别的意思吗？

2.为什么要祭祖？除了春节，还有什么时候祭祖？

3.上网查查看，郑成功(Zheng Cheng Gong)的生平。

http://history.cultural-china.com/en/47History2656.html

4.请说一说家谱（family tree）的意义。

5.请说一个你爷爷、奶奶、外公、外婆小时候的故事。

第五课

1.中文学校的春季学术比赛有哪些项目？

2.你在什么时候会感觉到孤单寂寞？

3.昨日歌（原本）的最后两四句是：水去日东流，花落日日少。成事立业在今日，莫待明朝悔今朝。请讨论它的含意。

4.有关时间的英文诗也很多，你最喜欢哪一首？请用中文说出它的大意。

第六课

1.为什么奶奶说晶晶对「人」有兴趣？

2 为什么说个性和命运是分不开的？

3.请上网去查查，耶鲁大学（Yale）还出了什么有名的中国人？

4.为什么西点军校的毕业生这么优秀？

Lesson One – Tears of Joy and Sorrow

Part One –

Cheng Wen's mother works at the International Architect Company as a senior architect. At the end of last year, the General Manager wanted to assign her to work at the Shanghai branch office for two years.   The total compensation provided by the company included: 1. a 30% increase in salary, plus year end bonus.   2. Company paid tuition and fees for two years for Cheng Wen.   3. Company paid apartment and rental car, and health and car insurance.   4. Company paid one-way airfare (business class) to Shanghai and a subsidy of one-half of the shipping cost for luggage (including air and sea).   5. Two weeks (ten working days) vacation per year to the United States, with company paid round-trip airfare for two (economy class).

Cheng Wen's mother figured that Shanghai is an international metropolis – full of vitality, the center of China's economy, trade and shipping industry, accessible from all parts of China by road and rail.   If they lived in Shanghai, she and Cheng Wen could visit different places in China frequently, even touring the Silk Road, to gain a deep understanding of Chinese history, art and culture. There were also many other advantages living in Shanghai, for example :   1.   The proximity to Taiwan would make it convenient to visit both her mother and parents-in-law there.   2.   With a higher salary and lower expenses, she could put away more savings each month.   3.   Their house in the U.S. could be leased and two years worth of rent would be a sizable income.   Figuring all these, there would be sufficient funds for Cheng Wen's college tuition.   4. There are international schools in Shanghai, with similar education systems and curricula as in the States.   It would not be a problem for students to go back to the U.S. to continue their education at any time.

However, Cheng Wen's mother did not immediately say yes to the General Manager as she needed to consider Cheng Wen's school transfer issues and to listen to Cheng Wen's opinion.

Part Two –

After getting home Cheng Wen's mother discussed the matter with Cheng Wen.   Not knowing what kind of city Shanghai was, Cheng Wen got on the internet to research information.   On the internet she saw the beautiful cityscape of Shanghai, its bustling streets, the unique architecture of the 2010 World Exposition, the Oriental Pearl Tower and the Memorial Monument built with 3000 railroad spikes, donated by the U.S. (the State of Illinois in 1991), commending the diligent and hardworking Chinese laborers who contributed to the building of the U.S. (the cross-continental railroads) in its early days.   Cheng Wen developed a deep interest in Shanghai, and she and her mother listed all the pros and cons of moving to Shanghai.   After two weeks of discussion and deliberation they finally opted to move to Shanghai.

During January, Cheng Wen downloaded the application forms of an international school on the internet.   She sent the completed forms, along with her photo, a copy of her passport and the application fee to the school.   Then her school, the Yuan Lin Middle School, mailed a recommendation letter and her transcript directly to the international school.   At the beginning of March, the school sent Cheng Wen a notification that she had been accepted.

Cheng Wen shed tears of both joy and sadness.   She was very happy going to Shanghai but couldn't bear to leave the States and her friends here.

Story for Lesson One: To Shanghai or Beijing?

1. Ever since making the decision to move to Shanghai, Cheng Wen became curious in the people, things and happenings in Shanghai.   One day, she read a very interesting story on the internet and shared it with her mother.

2. She said, "There were two peasants going to work in the city, one going to Beijing and the other to Shanghai.   They had bought their train tickets and sat in the waiting room to board their trains.   They heard some people chatting beside them …

3. One said, my second uncle visited Shanghai, and he had to pay someone just for directions. Another said, my aunt had no job in Beijing, but an old lady gave her steamed buns and used clothes, what a warm and friendly place.

4. The one going to Shanghai thought, Beijing was better, even if one could not find a job one would not starve to death!   The one going to Beijing thought, Shanghai was better, even those who gave direction to others could make money!

5. Both peasants changed their minds.   They met at the ticket counter, the one originally heading to Beijing got the ticket to Shanghai, while the one heading to Shanghai got the ticket to Beijing.

6. The one who went to Beijing discovered that Beijing was indeed good.   Bank lobbies offered free water for drinking at the water fountain, shopping centers offered free snacks for shoppers to sample.   He did not go hungry even without a job.

7. The one who went to Shanghai discovered that there were indeed lots of opportunities to make money in Shanghai: one could make money by guiding others to places or by attending restrooms.   One could make money as long as one used his mind and efforts.   He also discovered …

8. There were many skyscrapers in Shanghai, but very little greenery.   So he took advantage of his experience as a country folk by selling potted flowers and potted plants.   One year later, he rented a store front for his business, earning more and more money.   At this time he also discovered …

9. The outside walls of the skyscrapers were cleaned by cleaning companies, but they did not clean the shop signs.   Hence he bought step-ladders, buckets and rags to start his own business for cleaning sign boards.   Now he has more than one hundred workers.

10. Not long ago, he went to Beijing by train on business.   As soon as he got out of the train station he saw a drifter.   The two were dumbstruck at the sight of each other, because five years before, they had once exchanged their train tickets."   Cheng Wen finished her story and asked her mother's opinion.   Mother said:

11. "This is a fascinating story!   One's personality can determine one's destiny.   In each big city, such as New York and Chicago, there are workers from out of town to seek jobs.   Some are very diligent and create their own business while others become drifters."

12. Cheng Wen said: "I now understand personality is indeed very important.   Even if the two people had not changed their minds, even if they had not exchanged their tickets, the one who succeeded would still have succeeded, and the one who failed would still have failed." Mother said, "I agree with your view."

Lesson Two – Please Don't Ever Forget Me!

Part One –

Dear Pals,

After 14 hours of a long-distance flight, our flight arrived at the Shanghai International Airport at 2 PM yesterday.   In a spacious hall, we waited in line to go through immigration. When it was my turn, I handed to the immigration officer my passport, boarding pass* and the filled-out entrance registration form.   He asked me nicely the purpose of my China trip, while checking the visa in my passport.   I replied to him in Chinese and he kindly welcomed me to study in Shanghai wishing me best of luck.

Other than carry-on luggage, we had checked in two large heavy suitcases.   After we passed through immigration, we went to baggage claim to get our suitcases.   A fellow passenger from the same flight helped us remove our heavy suitcases from the conveyor belt and put them on the cart, which saved my mother and me a lot of trouble.

Aunt Mary brought her son Mike along to pick us up at the airport.   She said the company had booked a suite in Park Hotel for the first two nights, then we would move into our apartment afterwards.   The Park Hotel is very impressive, a famous five-star hotel in Shanghai (hotels here are called Fan-dien or Jiu-dien, terms for restaurants).   We got our room cards at the front desk, settled into the room, then went out to dinner together.   Aunt Mary insisted on treating us, saying it was a welcome dinner.

Mike is a sophomore in the American School.   He has been in Shanghai for a year and still speaks Mandarin with somewhat of a foreign accent.   He can only speak one sentence in Shanghainese, that is, I thank you.   Mike is a warm and cheerful guy, who can carry on quite a conversation and we had a great time chatting.

Dear all, please email me often and don't ever forget your friend in Shanghai!

Sincerely,

Cheng Wen

Part Two –

Dear Cheng Wen,

The day my mother and I went to the airport to see you off, we were delayed for an hour by a major accident on the highway.   By the time we arrived at the airport, you had already gone through security and entered the departure lounge.   What a pity to have missed you!

School has already started for us.   Mrs. Lee, my guidance counselor, arranged a meeting with me before school started, to assist me with the curriculum of my four years of high school.   She was concerned about the curriculum of my four years of high school.   I said I would like to take more AP classes because good AP exam scores not only would be recognized as college credits but also provided a better chance to get into name schools. She asked me about my future career interests.   I said I would like to work in the public sector, such as a school district commissioner, city council or a mayor (LOL!).   Mrs. Lee said: "Excellent!" and suggested I join the school debating club.

This semester, I am continuing with Chinese school and also preparing for the Chinese SAT exam at the beginning of November.   Our Chinese class Teacher Xu said that recently Lakers' Kobe Bryant supported the offering of Kong-fu classes at three L.A. high schools. The Kong-fu teacher teaches the students to shout out the commands in Chinese, so that students exercise while practicing Chinese, killing two birds with one stone.   So Teacher Xu also leads us in the "Five Animal Exercise" in Chinese class, making us shout out the Kong-fu commands in Chinese, with pretty decent results.   Till next time!
Yours, Ming-Ming

Story for Lesson Two: Physical Fitness Qi-gong: Five-Animal Exercise

(Teachers, please lead the students in doing the Five Animal Exercise in class.   All the commands are on page123-126 of the textbook.   You can also find the exercise video on line, provided by www.mzchinese.org)

1. Wu Qiang is a martial arts master.   He knows all kinds of hand combat moves as well as use of weapons, and often serves as the martial arts director for Kong-fu action movies. Everyone is happy that he agreed to teach the Kong-fu class at our Chinese school.
2. We all gathered in the indoor gym to welcome him.   He told us a joke as soon as he got on the stage: There were three Kong-fu masters having tea together and a few bugs were flying around.   The first master drew out his Samurai sword, brandished it twice, and a fly fell to the ground.
3. Lo and behold, the fly was cut into three pieces.   Unconvinced, the second master drew out his fencing sword, brandished it twice, another fly fell to the ground.   Wow!   The two rows of its feet were gone.   At this moment, a mosquito flew by, the third man picked up a tooth pick from the table,
4. stabbed it twice in the air, and the mosquito quickly stopped on the glass table top.   Taking a closer look, wow, the mosquito was looking at itself in the mirror; as a matter of fact it now had double-fold eyelids!"   Everyone was rolling on the floor laughing after hearing this! Teacher Wu said, "The purpose of learning martial arts is not …
5. for harming others, but for physical fitness and self defense.   Today I am going to teach you "Five Animal Exercise", a kind of Qi-gong for physical fitness.   Invented by the great Chinese physician, Hua Tuo, 2000 years ago, it imitates the movements of five animals: tiger, deer, bear, ape, and bird.
6. Nowadays it has been simplified into ten movements, thus very easy to learn.   Teacher Wu continued: "First, follow me in reciting the commands in Chinese.   Do the movement while you say it out loud, which will keep you focused.   After saying a few times out loud you can do it in silence.   What's more, before you practice the movements of the Five Animal Exercise,

7. you should begin with the starting form and end with the closing form." After finishing his explanation, Teacher Wu started leading everyone with the command of the starting form. Everyone recited his commands and moved at the same time: "Two feet apart, shoulder width; eyes forward, slightly bend your knees; abs in, relax the whole body.

8. Inhale slowly, arms up slowly in front, palms down. Raise hands slowly to shoulder height, turn palms toward each other, fold them on the chest. Slowly push down towards the abs, to 3 inches below your belly button, exhale at the same time." Then Teacher Wu invited several students who had learned Kong-fu up to the stage to demonstrate.

9. Therefore, John and six or seven students who had learned Judo, Tae Kwon Do, Shaolin or Taichi got on the stage. They had some martial arts foundation, therefore picked up the movements very quickly. They performed the movements of Tiger Swooping, Fawn Running, Bear Walking,

10. Monkey Peach-picking, and Large Bird Taking-off. While everyone was watching intently, John, who was on the stage, suddenly changed his hands into tiger claws and swooped down at Teacher Wu. Teacher Wu quickly took one step back, while John's face was almost at the floor,

11. Teacher Wu gently raised his foot and straightened John up. Everyone was awed with admiration. Teacher Wu said with a smile, "Try not to rush! There are three secrets to learning the Five Animal Exercise. First, imagine yourself as a courageous and ferocious tiger, …

12. a calm and peaceful deer, a strong bear, a mischievous monkey and an agile bird. Second, recite the commands in Chinese. Third, exercise persistence and perseverance. If you follow these, you will benefit endlessly.

Lesson Three Text – Dear Journal, Thank you!

Part One –   November 15th

Dear Diary,

Mom and I have moved to Shanghai for three months now. I unpacked the books and other miscellaneous items that were shipped by sea to put them away, and saw the diary that Dad gave me where it contained my childhood life from nine to eleven years old.

During the year when I was ten, Dad often had an upset stomach, especially before and after meals. At the beginning, he thought it was indigestion caused by high stress at work. Later the family doctor suggested he consult an internist, and the results of the examination turned out to be liver cancer that had progressed to late stages. The surgeon operated on Dad, excising part of the liver in a fairly successful surgery. Subsequently, oncologists began chemotherapy and radiation for him. Every day, Dad had to take medicine, receive injections, and frequently had his blood pressure measured, blood tested, urine checked, and X-rays taken. During that time, Dad was miserable – he often suffered headaches, fever, vomiting, diarrhea, even stomatitis (inflammation inside the mouth). His immunity was very weak – every time he sneezed, coughed or had a runny nose, Mom got very nervous. If Dad caught a cold or got infected with the flu, his symptoms were more severe than most people, necessitating a ride in the ambulance for a trip to the emergency room. He checked into the hospital often.　The doctors and nurses all said he was the most cooperative patient, he was good tempered and never complained or troubled others.When it became apparent that western medicine was not going to cure his disease, Dad subsequently sought help from Chinese doctors and took Chinese herbal medicine.　This dragged things out for another month but Dad still left us.

I very much treasure the times I spent next to Dad's sick bed, which I recorded in detail in my journal.　My journal shared my happiness, sadness and hopes.　Thanks to frequently writing a journal, I discovered that I have improved my ability in writing, expressing and thinking.　I also discovered that writing a journal has been good to my mental health. My dear diary, thank you very much.

Part Two –　　　　　　　　　　　　　　　　　　　November 23rd
Dear Diary,

Zhong-Zhong wrote in a letter I received today that he participated in the American Cancer Society's 'Relay for Life' event last weekend.　I used to participate in it every year. We first raised money from our family and friends and last year we raised a total of $1,200. On the day of the event, we stayed in a tent and took turns to walk around the track field for 24 hours without stop, to convey that the movement to overcome and prevent cancer would also never end.　My favorite part used to be the lantern lighting program at night.　Everyone could write the names of those they want to remember or pray for in their hearts on small paper bags and light a light inside.　Over a thousand paper bags surrounded the tracks, with a big 'HOPE' arranged on the stands – this was quite a spectacle!

During Dad's illness, volunteers from the American Cancer Society gave us a lot of help, comfort and encouragement.　'Relay for life' is one of the major events of ACS, in which millions participate every year, with everyone contributing to the eradication and prevention of cancer as the common goal.

When I chatted with Mike today, he said there was also 'Relay for Life' at the American School in Shanghai.　Just like in the U.S., participating high school students can receive points for community service.　I am really glad I can still continue to participate in this activity in China.

Lesson Three Story – 4000 km Bicycle Ride

1. Cancer is the biggest enemy to human health.　It should be everyone's responsibility to fight and prevent cancer.　There has been a moving real-life story occurred in northern California: several years ago, there was an optimistic, enterprising, vivacious and friendly girl named Yang Qi-Wen.
2. One day, she found a small lump in her leg.　The doctor diagnosed it as muscle cancer, with the situation not very optimistic.　Qi-wen's mother was very sad.　Qi-wen comforted her, saying she would face her illness bravely.　She was in Grade 11 that year.

3. Qi-wen had undergone many operations and numerous chemotherapy sessions. She often suffered vomiting, fever, pain and even hair loss. Her classmates pushed her around in her wheelchair, helped her with homework, and even folded paper cranes to wish her good health and longevity.

4. They organized teams to participate in "Relay for Life" events with Qi-wen. The teachers and students at Silicon Valley Chinese School also responded to this event, showing their support for Qi-wen's determination to overcome cancer with their action. Qi-wen persisted in diligently pursuing her studies. After graduating from Saratoga High School,

5. Qi-wen entered UC Berkeley and her best friend, Guo Jie-xin, entered Boston University. A year later, as cancer cells spread to her lungs and her entire body. At that time, to encourage Qi-wen, Jie-xin, who was never physically strong and did not like sports, bravely signed up

6. the cancer fighting bike tour from the east coast to the Golden Gate Bridge. She thought that if Qi-wen saw she did it, then Qi-wen would have more courage to fight the cancer. Qi-wen was moved to tears, saying she would welcome them back at the Golden Gate Bridge!

7. Just before Christmas, Qi-wen was hospitalized. Her classmates hurried back home, taking turns to keep her company. They joked around with Qi-wen in soft voices to keep her spirits up. Jie-xin asked Qi-wen, "Can I still ride for you?" Qi-wen nodded with a smile. A few days later, Qi-wen passed away and she was only 19.

8. Qi-wen liked paper cranes the best. At the memorial service with more than 200 in attendance, Qi-wen's classmates bid her farewell with musical instruments, songs, flowers and 400 paper cranes. They wanted to turn their friendship for Qi-wen into love for the mass, to support research and actions to fight and prevent cancer.

9. Jie-xin trained physically while collecting contributions for the 4000 km bicycle ride. She succeeded in collecting $10,000! The contribution would be used to build a "HOPE Hut", dedicated to accommodating cancer patients who could not afford to stay in hospitals.

10. The summer break came! On the early morning of May 28th, Jie-xin, Lin Zhuo-min and other team members gathered at the shore at Baltimore. They dipped the rear wheels of their bikes in the Atlantic Ocean and began a journey that went through the wind, the rain, the hot sun, sleeping in tents and lying on the ground.

11. They travelled through 13 states, encouraging the patients in cancer centers along the way. They crossed over three major mountain ranges and traversed the great Nevada desert, encountering many close calls but no real danger. Sixty-two days later, they finally arrived at the Golden Gate Bridge at the edge of the Pacific.

12. The team members put the front wheels of their bicycles into the Pacific Ocean, with shouts of excitement! At that moment, Jie-xin raised her head and looking at the blue sky, she murmured in her heart, "Qi-wen, I have done it, for you and the cause of preventing and fighting cancer. You must be very pleased!"

Lesson Four Text – Celebrating Chinese New Year in Taiwan

Part One –

It is almost the Chinese New Year (also known as the Spring Festival)! Cheng Wen and Mom flew back to grandpa and grandma's house in Taipei to celebrate the Chinese New Year.

During the three days before the Chinese New Year, they accompanied Grandma to Di-Hua Street to purchase New Year's supplies.   Every store front had heaps of various dry goods and seasonal candied sweets, with customers coming and going in a continuous stream, in quite a hustle and bustle!   Mom bought various dry foods such as Shitake mushrooms, scallops, sea cucumbers, tree ears, salted fish, dried shrimps and Chinese sausages; various seasonings such as sesame seed oil, soy sauce, dried citrus peel, Chinese cinnamon, hot pepper powder and pepper; in addition, various snacks such as five-spice watermelon seeds, spicy dried bean curd and sesame candies, followed by a taxi ride home in high spirits.

As soon as they arrived home they saw the bright red Spring Festival couplets just put up by grandpa, with the character 'Fortune' pasted upside-down on the front door.   Showing her sophistication (in Chinese culture), Cheng Wen purposely said out loud, "Good fortune has arrived!"   Indeed Grandma followed with a smile, "Exactly!   Fortune has arrived!   Fortune has arrived!"

The thirtieth of the twelfth Lunar month is New Years Eve.   Uncle's entire family hurried home from Taizhong, boosting the festival atmosphere at home even more.   Before the New Year Eve's dinner, everyone arranged the ten dishes such as sweet & sour fish in front of the ancestor tablets (inscribed with the family or ancestor names).   Grandpa then offered incense and wine, followed by everyone bowing respectfully in unison.   Grandpa said, "Ancestor worship is the traditional culture of China, and carries the meaning of remembering one's roots."

The entire family gathered together for the New Year Eve dinner!   [Editor's note – 围炉 means to gather around the family hearth, an ancient tradition the expression of which still refers to New Year's Eve dinner.]   In addition to New Year dishes there was a steamy hot pot. After dinner, uncle, aunt and Mom took out red envelops, first offering to grandpa and grandma with respect, then passed out New Year's gift money to the children.   Cheng Wen received five red envelops, instantly becoming a little rich lady.   When dinner was over, Cheng Wen stayed up with the adults to bring in the New Year.   At midnight, there came the sounds of firecrackers.   Cheng Wen happily shouted, "New Year is here!   Wish everyone a prosperous new year!"

On New Year's morning, the children greeted the elders Happy New Year with a bow. There were boiled Chinese dumplings, glutinous rice cake and radish cake for breakfast, which represented good luck year after year, rising up to new heights year after year.

Part Two –
The second day of the New Year is the day for married women to return to their birth families.   Early morning, Cheng Wen and mother brought big and small packets of gifts, and hurried to grandmother's house in Tainan.   As soon as they entered the door they saw a

table full of food.   Auntie said that the rice noodle with meat sauce, fish head in a clay pot and boiled salted duck were all made by Grandmother herself.   Cheng Wen felt Grandmother's deep love.

In the afternoon, uncle's daughter Shi-Mei, an elder cousin, accompanied Cheng Wen to stroll around the city.   Tainan was an ancient cultural city, they visited the Confucius Temple and the An-ping Old Fort (built by the Dutch in 1624, the oldest fort on Taiwan), and in front of the Fort was a stone statue of Zheng Cheng-gong.   Cousin said, "Over three hundred years ago, Zheng Cheng-gong led armies to invade Taiwan and expelled the Dutch who had occupied it for 38 years.   Subsequently, people from Fujian and Guangdong provinces were able to sail across the sea in large numbers, to live in peace and prosperity here.   Although Taiwan was later occupied again by the Japanese for 50 years (1895 to 1945 ending with WWII), the Chinese traditional culture had taken deep roots among the common folk over hundreds of years."

Cheng Wen said, "My mother said according to our family tree, uncles is the 56th generation grandson of the Chen family from Henan province, the 8th generation in Taiwan." Cousin said, "Correct, my Dad and your Mom, my aunt, their name belongs to the 'Yuan' generation.   My elder brother, I and my younger cousin belong to the generation with 'Shi' in our names.   The generation name is arranged based on a passage in the family tree: 'Honesty and kindness carry the family far, knowledge and learning perpetuate the generations long'."   Cheng Wen said, "I will also compile a family tree for my descendents, stipulating that those from the same generation will use the same Chinese Pinyin as their middle name."   Cousin teased her, "No rush!   No rush!   On the 7th day of the 7th Lunar month (Chinese Valentine's Day), grandmother will hold a Sweet Sixteen Adult Initiation Rite for you.   After all, you must first become an adult before you can be married, right?"

Lesson Four Story – You-you at a Wedding Party

1. Today was the day Lin You-qiang and Huang Zheng-xiang got married.   You-qiang is You-you's cousin, the eldest grandson of their grandparents.   Today's wedding ceremony was held in a Catholic church, and an evening banquet was given for their relatives and friends at the Seafood Restaurant in Chinatown.

2. At the entrance of the restaurant, big red characters of "the Lin Family and Huang Family Wedding Banquet" were shown on the billboard.   Dressed in splendid attire, guests arrived with joyful spirits, some carrying gifts while others brining cash.   After signing their names, they handed the gifts to the receptionists.

3. Grandfather, uncle and aunt, as well as the bride's parents were seated at the main table, as they were masters of the wedding ceremony.   All the guests at You-you's table were young people.   You-qiang had asked the waitress to take special care of them.   Before the meal, the masters of the wedding ceremony delivered their speeches, giving many blessings to the bride and groom.

4. The dishes were served!   The waitress said: "There are altogether ten dishes, representing 100% perfection in every way."   She put the first dish on the Lazy Susan and

said, "This assorted cold dish contains chicken, duck, fish, beef, jellyfish, seaweed and sausages.   They should whet your appetite.   Please take your time!"

5. Everyone was ill at ease to be the first to take the food.   The waitress said, "There is no guest of honor or any elders at your table.   Whoever happens to sit in front of the dish can start, and turn the Lazy-Susan clockwise so everyone can take turns."

6. After the assorted cold dish came the soup.   She said, "This is shark's fin soup.   Shark's fin is very nutritious, rare and expensive.   But shark's fin can no longer be sold in Hawaii. Perhaps it will also not be allowed for sale locally.   Please give it a try!"   Thus …

7. the protection of sharks became a hot topic of conversation.   At this time, the waitress brought a plate of crispy chicken and a small dish of peppered salt.   She said, "This dish tastes better if you dip the chicken in the peppered salt.   Please try!"   So everybody stood up, eating while continuing talking.

8. The manager saw this from afar, hurried over and asked: "Do you need any help?" Everyone said, "No, not at all!"   The manager said, "Then please be seated, please sit down and eat!"   They all sat down.   A short while later, the waitress came and reminded everyone again that the chicken should be dipped with the peppered salt.

9. You-you said, "You told us to stand up and eat, but the manager asked us to sit down. How should we eat?"   With a smile, the waitress picked up a piece of chicken, dipped it in the spiced salt and said, "Dip".   You-you said in embarrassment, "Ah!   We misunderstood you."

10. At this time, the bride and the groom came over to give a toast.   Everyone hurriedly stood up, raised their glasses and said, "We will drink juice in lieu of wine and wish you great happiness through all your life."   The bride and the groom said, "Thanks for your blessings!"

11. After several other dishes, the waitress brought over a large plate of fried rice with salted fish and ham and said, "This is the last dish, the staple food (which is usually rice, pasta, potato, a starchy food that we eat with every meal)."   After a little while, she also brought over fruit, cake and rice dumplings stuffed with red bean paste.

12. The waitress pointed to the dumplings and said, "The dessert is courtesy of our manager who expresses his wish to the newlyweds and all of you of great happiness and success." Everyone felt very happy.   You-you and the guests raised their glasses to thank the waitress for her attentive service.

Lesson Five Text – Poetry Reciting Contest

The Association of Chinese Schools is about to hold a spring academic contest.   The contest includes competition in Calligraphy (Brush category, Non-brush category), Chinese Traditional Painting, Speech, and Poetry Reciting (Individuals – limited to assigned poems, Groups – self selected poems).   Qing-Qing's class plans to participate in the Poetry Recital Group competition.

Teacher Xu asked everyone what poems they wanted to recite.   Qing-Qing said she had learned a Tang Dynasty poem named 'Ascending the You-Zhou Tower' and wasn't sure if it would be appropriate.   Teacher Xu said, "You-Zhou is today's Beijing, which was very desolate in the Tang dynasty.   At that time, Chen Zi-Ang came to this place with the army while fighting a war.   He often felt dejected, regretful and depressed.   One day, he wanted to go up to You-Zhou Tower to view the scenery and relieve his weariness.   But when he ascended to the top and looked out in the distance, he was instead overtaken by a confluence of emotions, with a deep sorrow rising from within, thus he took out his brush and wrote this great work of the ages.   In the poem, the eternity of heaven and earth was set off by the loneliness and shortness of life; in plain and concise language he expressed the common sorrow of mankind.   Therefore, this poem is especially moving and thought provoking, making us deeply ponder the meaning and value our life.

Teacher Xu went on, "For the competition, you will use this poem and additionally 'Song of Today' and 'Song of Tomorrow', which remind folks to cherish time.   These three poems together are nearly perfect."   Zhong-Zhong asked, "Are the other two new poems and songs?"   Teacher Xu said, "No, they were written by poets from the Ming and Qing dynasties. You probably have no idea of the sequence of Chinese dynasties, so let me teach you a 'Song of Dynasties'!"

Ascending You-Zhou Tower by Chen Zi-Ang, Tang Dynasty (the city gate tower of ancient Beijing)

I do not see ancients in front of me,
I do not see followers in back of me,
Reflecting on the eternity of heaven and earth,
With loneliness and sorrow, my tears come streaming down.

Poem of Today by Wen Jia, a painter of Ming dynasty

Today and another today,
There are so few todays!
If again not done today,
When can the matter at hand be finished?
How many todays are there in a lifetime,
What a pity if it is not done today.
If you say wait till tomorrow,
Tomorrow has tomorrow's business.
Compose for thee a simple poem of today,
Please start your effort from today.

Song of Tomorrow by Qian Fu-Hua, Ming dynasty

Tomorrow and another tomorrow,
There are so many tomorrows!
If I wait for tomorrow my entire life,
Everything will idle away.
We on earth are painfully burdened by tomorrows,
Spring followed by autumn we will soon be old.
Mornings we watch the river flow to the east,
Evenings we watch the sun set in the west.

How much can a hundred years of tomorrows amount to?
Please heed my song of tomorrow.

Song of Dynasties
Yan Huang, Yao, Shun, Xia, Shang, and Zhou,
Spring and Autumn, The Warring States, so chaotic you don't want to know!
After Qin and Han, came The Three Kingdoms, united by Jin,
The Southern and the Northern Dynasties, opposed, all wanting to be the only King.
Then came along Sui, Tang, the Five Dynasties and the Ten Kingdoms,
Song, Yuan, Ming and Qing, that finished off all the emperors' fun.

Lesson Five Story – Chinese History

1. Chinese culture originated in the Yellow River region.   Archaeologists discovered that more than seven thousand years ago, Chinese people already knew how to make colored earth ware.   More than four thousand years ago, Yandi (Fire Emperor Shen-Nong) taught the people how to cultivate mountains and till the land.   Subsequently, Huangdi (Yellow Emperor) united all the tribes.

2. Leizu (Huangdi's wife) invented silk making, Cang Jie created Chinese characters, and the Chinese culture gradually came into being.   When it was around 2000 BC, Shun gave his throne to the great Yu, because of Yu's achievements in flood control (by regulating rivers and waterways).   Yu passed the throne to his son and established the very first dynasty of China name Xia.   Thus native or overseas Chinese

3. often call themselves Yan Huang descendants and Hua Xia nation.   Ho Yi, of the legend of Chang-e flying to the moon, had even been an emperor of the Xia Dynasty for a few years. After Xia came the Shang Dynasty, during which time people invented ox and horse drawn carts and the use of copper and shells as currency for doing business.

4. That's why characters such as to buy, to sell, wealth, commodity, expensive, cheap, treasure … all contain the character (or radical) "shell".   The Zhou Dynasty that followed Shang established a social class system, with etiquette and ritual ceremonies.   In 770 BC, the Zhou Dynasty was divided into many small states, thus began the highly competitive

5. Spring and Autumn and the Warring States period.   This period saw a great many thinker philosophers, political scientists, educators, military strategists, engineers, such as Confucius, Lao-zi, Sun-zi, Lu Ban, Qu Yuan, etc.   Further, science and technology also greatly advanced.   In medicine, weaponry, machinery, mathematics,

6. construction and architecture and irrigation engineering, there were many inventions, including the multiplication table and the Chinese chess with which we are all familiar.   In 221BC, Qin Shi Huang (the First Emperor of the Qin Dynasty) united the entire country, and standardized the written language, currency, the width between the wheels (of carts), weights and measures,

7. as well as built the Great Wall.   After Qin came the Han Dynasty, which expanded the Silk Road, furthering dealings and contact with the West.   'Standard Script' became the common style of writing throughout the country.   Han is a strong and powerful empire,

8. its major inventions include the abacus, papermaking, gunpowder, acupuncture, porcelain, the seismograph, etc.   After the breakup of the Han Dynasty began the era of the Three Kingdoms, Western and Eastern Jin, and the Southern and Northern Dynasties.   More than three hundred years of war and turmoil brought about the great integration of the Chinese peoples.

9. Guan Gong (Guan Yu), widely worshipped by the common folks, and Zu Chong-zhi, inventor of the way to precisely calculate the ratio of circumference of a circle to its diameter, were both figures from this period.   After that, the Sui Dynasty unified China, opened up the Grand Canal that connected north and south (the Yellow River basin and the Yangtze River basin), and established the first civil examination system in the world.

10. Following Sui was the Tang Dynasty, which achieved great achievements in culture, economy, politics, military strength, diplomacy, literature, fine arts, science, poetry, etc.   Tang Dynasty spread (?) China's fame throughout the world.   The poem 'Reflection in a Quiet Night', familiar to all children,

11. was composed by the great poet Li Bai in the Tang Dynasty.   After Tang, the country was divided into Five Dynasties and Ten States, and the Chinese people once again went through a great integration.   Then was the Song Dynasty.   With a smaller territory, the Song Dynasty could not but develop maritime transport and trade, as well as pursue advances in agriculture, science and technology, medicine, ship-building, etc. The Song Dynasty.....

12. turned block printing into movable-type, the southward pointing instrument into the compass, and the gunpowder into the cannon, bringing utilitarian function of these technologies into full play and influenced world civilization.   In 1271AD, the Mongolians unified China and established the Yuan Dynasty, becoming

13. the dynasty that occupied the largest territory in the history of China.   Marco Polo came to China during that time; his travel notes *The Travels of Marco Polo*" stimulated the Westerners' longing for China.   After that, the Ming Dynasty succeeded the Yuan Dynasty. The greatest person in the Ming Dynasty was Zheng He, who for seven times led a flotilla of thousands of ships that travelled afar,

14. to Malaysia, India, Persia (modern Iran) and the east coast of Africa.   Regrettably,   the Ming emperor burned all ships and forbade ocean sailing after that.   At this time, the industrial revolution in Europe accelerated the modernization of the Western world.   In 1616 AD, the Manchurians defeated the Ming Dynasty,

15. and founded the Qing Dynasty.   The Qing Dynasty closed its border and imposed self isolation, not paying attention to the development of science and technology.   China soon fell behind Europe.   After China was defeated in the Opium War in 1840, Great Britain, France, Russia, Japan, Germany and Portugal repeatedly invaded China,

16. occupied China's territory, and robbed mineral resources, treasures and wealth.   In the short span of sixty years, China lost a quarter of its territory.   The Chinese people became very poor and had to risk going overseas to perform menial labor as Chinese coolies.   They became the earliest Chinese immigrants to various countries in the world.   In 1912,

17. the Republic of China was founded, overturning the dynasty system that had lasted for thousands of years in China.   In 1937, Japan found an excuse to invade China and after

eight years of war, in 1945, Japan surrendered and returned Taiwan and Peng Hu Islands to China.   Soon after, the China Civil War erupted.

18. In 1949, the People's Republic of China was founded in Beijing, which ruled mainland China, and the government of the Republic of China moved to Taiwan.   Today, the peoples of Mainland and Taiwan have mutual contact, with ever more intimate exchange of economic, cultural, trade and other relations.

Lesson Six Text – I Like Both Colleges

Part One –

Jing-jing, Ming-ming's elder sister, is an eleventh grader who will be applying to colleges after the summer.   Jing-jing is very interested in Yale University and West Point.   Thus they took advantage of the three-day Memorial holiday weekend and accompanied Jing-jing to visit these two schools and their dormitories.   Afterwards they went to New York City to visit grandma and auntie's family.

After supper, grandma and Jing-jing sat on the sofa chatting.   Grandma asked her what she planned to major in.   Jing-jing said, "I haven't decided yet, but I am interested in such subjects as psychology, sociology and education."   Grandma said, "In that case, your interests are not 'things' but rather 'people'."   Jing-jing said, "Yes, I am very interested in the topics of human personality and emotions, for example, the relationship between personality and heredity, how to manage emotions and control temper, etc."   Grandma said, "Hmm, these are indeed worth studying, as personality and destiny are inseparable.   Personality is made up of many things, for example, optimism, pessimism, introvert, extrovert, self-discipline, willfulness, irritability, cool-headedness, greed, contentment, tolerance, fastidiousness, vivaciousness, shyness, …"   Jing-jing asked, "Grandma, are you reciting antonyms?"   Grandma smiled, "Don't interrupt!   Do you know – if one develops a personality of self-confidence, kind heartedness and humor, one is likely to be much happier?   If one is often anxious, depressed, angry, jealous or suspicious, then his emotional health must not be good."   Jing-jing said, "In that case, we should pay attention to how we feel all the time, observing and analyzing the changes in our feelings, so that we can find ways to improve. Correct?"   Grandma said, "Absolutely …"   As they were eagerly chatting, Ming-ming walked by and purposely sat next to grandma and said, "Grandma, my sister loathes to be asked about her college plans.   She feels pressure.   Whenever someone brings up college, she gets impatient.   Consequently even Mom and Dad don't ask about it."   Jing-jing hurriedly said, "Oh, grandma is naturally different!   Don't you come and cause trouble!"   Grandma laughed!

Part Two –

Grandma again asked Jing-jing's thoughts on the school visits.   Jing-jing said, "The students at West Point are full of vigor.   Their creed is: duty, honor, purpose, courage, competitiveness, passion, obedience, respect, loyalty, etc."   Grandma said, "If possessed with this kind of character, one will naturally succeed!   No wonder according to the newspapers, many heads in the business world are graduates of West Point!"   Grandma asked further, "Yale University is classical and pretty, filled with an air of the humanities. Do you like Yale?" Jing-jing said, "I do. Yale's creed is 'truth and light'. In front of the library, there is a Women's Table that commemorates the role of women at Yale, a work by Maya Lin (who won the competition with her design of the Vietnam Veterans Memorial in Washington DC). In the hall of famous alumni are displayed the very first overseas Chinese student Rong Hong, as well as several portraits of U.S. presidents such as Bush and Clinton. Grandma, I really like these two schools, but it is not easy to be admitted!" Grandma said with light hearted humor, "Worry not, just do your best. Our Jing-jing is so outstanding that it will be the good fortune of whichever college that can have her, otherwise it is their loss!" Everyone laughed, "Go, Jing-jing, go!"

Lesson Six Story – The Story of Maya Ying Lin

1. Teacher Chen brought her students to visit Washington DC last summer. While everyone sat on the lawn to have lunch, she pointed to the distance and said, "Look! That is the Vietnam Memorial designed by Lin Ying, or Maya Ying Lin. She is a legendary character.

2. Maya Lin's parents were overseas students from China who later served as professors at the University of Ohio. In 1959, Maya was born in Athens. At that time, they were the only Chinese family in the area. From childhood Maya enjoyed an intimate life with her family of four, her dad, mom and an older brother.

3. Maya had an introverted personality and loved to read since she was little. She was a favorite of teachers and a little bookworm in the eyes of classmates. She liked math and drawing. After high school graduation, she was accepted by the School of Architecture of Yale University. She was very happy there, like fish in water.

4. It was a time not too long after the Vietnam War ended. America suffered a great loss of 58,000 soldiers killed in action and 350,000 injured, and many veterans had no work. Feelings of conflict, disappointment and anger were pervasive in the society.

5. At that time, the veterans suggested building a Vietnam Memorial in Washington DC, to affirm the contribution of the soldiers for their country. This proposal received wide spread resonance from the entire country. In 1980, the organizing committee of the Vietnam Memorial began soliciting design proposals nationwide.

6. Maya became very interested. The traditional memorials at the time were mostly white structures or statues, but Maya's design cut into the earth and erected two shiny black stone walls shaped as a "V" on which was carved every soldier's name in the chronological order of their death in battle.

7. Her professor encouraged her to submit her design. Of the 1,421 anonymous proposals submitted throughout the country, Maya Lin's design was selected. This event caused a great sensation in the country, but many veterans opposed her design, and loathed her Asian origin even more.

8. Through media reporting, the whole thing got out of hand. Even President Reagan, the Secretary of the Interior, and many prominent congressmen were opposed to it. What was Maya going to do? Surprisingly, the 21 year old Maya was not intimidated.

9. While facing down pressure and discrimination with courage, she also worked hard to fight

for everyone's support.   She telephoned the Vice President, wrote letters to architecture reviewers and went on to TV programs to explain the ideas behind the design of her memorial.

10. At Congressional hearings, the opposing party requested the installation of American flags and the erection of bronze statues.   Maya was adamantly against it and finally they removed the US flags and bronze statues.   The construction of the Memorial thus began.   Would the American people accept this design that broke from tradition?   Everyone was waiting and watching.

11. The voices of criticism never ceased.   She felt very lonely so she returned to Yale Graduate School, to pursue further studies.   The Memorial was completed in 1982.   Tens of thousands took part in the inauguration, during which there was no one who dared to bring up Maya Lin's name!

12.But the Memorial moved people to wails and tears.   They recalled Maya's words, 'When people read or touch with their own hands the names of their loved ones or comrades, the grief would burst out like an explosion.   Only when people face grief,

13. can they walk out of it and begin a new life.   This was my original intent for designing the Memorial.'   After the Memorial was built, millions came to visit every year.   People call it the Healing Wall, one of the ten most popular architecture sites in America."

14. Jing-Jing asked, "What happened to Maya Lin after that?"   Teacher Chen said, "Her talents were affirmed and she created more famous works.   Today Maya is an internationally famous architect and artist.   The American people are proud of her and reporters also interview her often.

15. Although Maya Lin became a celebrity, her manners are still modest, gentle, and practical. She said her outlook on life was influenced by her family upbringing and Chinese culture. Her creations embraced eastern and western cultures.

16. She let her two daughters learn Chinese, hoping they would learn Chinese culture.   To preserve the historical artifacts of Chinese American immigrants, the Museum of Chinese Americans (MOCA) designed by Maya Lin for New York City has been completed and inaugurated in 2009.

17. Maya Lin's work is filled with the idea that man is an integral part of nature.   Nowadays, she is even more focused on works that protect the natural environment."   After teacher Chen finished the story of Maya Lin, everyone visited the Vietnam Memorial.   Jing-Jing saw herself on the shiny wall,

18.and walls full of names floating among the crowds, trees, the blue sky and white clouds. In front of them was the Washington Monument and behind them was the Lincoln Memorial. Jing-Jing felt as if they were watching over those killed in action while reminding everyone: Country, Honor and Duty.   What a marvelous design!   What a genius is Maya!

五禽戏

一、 手形

	**虎戏**：虎戏的手形是虎爪，五指张开，第一、二指关节向内弯曲，模拟老虎的利爪。
	**猿戏**：猿戏的手形是猿钩，五指撮拢，手腕向下弯。
	**鹿戏**：鹿戏的手形是鹿角，中指、无名指 弯曲，其余三指伸直张开。
	**熊戏**：熊戏的手形是熊掌，手指弯曲，大拇指压在食指、中指的指节上，虎口撑圆。
	鸟戏：鸟戏的手形是鸟翅，中指和无名指向下，其余三指向上翘。

二、口令:

虎戏

	*虎举* 1. 掌心朝下，十指张开， 从小指开始按照次序将关节弯曲握拳。 2. 双手提起到胸前，手指慢慢松开、掌心向上高举。 3. 由小指起依次将关节弯曲握拳，下拉至胸前，再变掌，掌心朝下，十指张开，往下按。

虎扑

1. 两手握空拳从身体两侧上提，

2. 两手前伸变虎爪，上身向前弯，背平，屁股往后。

3. 虎爪下按至膝，弯膝，握空拳上提，同时，髋部(小腹)向前，身体后仰。

4. 双手变虎爪下扑，同时，左脚向前，屁股后坐。

猿戏

猿提
1. 两臂下垂，手放在身前，十指张开，快速捏拢成猿钩
2. 肩上耸，缩脖，双手提到胸前。
3. 收腹提肛，脚跟提起。
4. 头向左转，眼向左看。
5. 头转回，肩放松，松腹落肛，脚跟着地，身体放松，姿态还原。
6. 重复同样动作做右式

猿摘

1. 右手弯曲放在腰间，重心在左脚，右脚向右后方退一步，

2. 重心从左脚移到右脚，同时左手画弧，停在头右前上方

3. 收左脚成丁步，转头看左前上方

4. 左手下按，身体下蹲，左脚向左后方退一步，

5. 扭身，重心移到左脚，同时右手向左上方伸展，手形变钩

6. 右手收回，手心向上像捧桃样，左手下托，左脚收回成丁步

鹿戏

鹿抵

1. 左脚上抬后向前一步, 重心在右脚。

2. 收腹、背圆、肩膀向前, 两臂前伸双手变鹿角, 手背相对。

3. 头在两手臂中间, 眼睛往下看, 重心向后坐。

鹿奔

1. 两膝微曲, 重心右移,

2. 左脚提起向右前方着地, 脚尖外转 90 度, 屈膝, 右腿拉直,

3. 身体稍前倾, 腰向左旋转

4. 握空拳, 两臂向右侧摆起, 与肩等高时, 空拳变鹿角, 随身左转。

5. 左手肘在腰部, 右手往后伸, 眼睛看右脚后跟。

6. 重心右移, 前脚收回。

熊戏

熊运

1. 两脚分开和肩膀同宽, 上身稍前俯。

2. 两臂放松, 双手变熊掌放在小肚子前。

3. 身体向右→上→左→下画圆圈, 跨骨不跟着动。

4. 腰和肚子有压紧和放松的感觉。

熊晃

1. 提髋，屈腿，身体自然下压，向前跨步，膝踝关节放松整个脚掌着地

2. 身体后坐，再前靠，两只手一前一后随着身体摆动

3. 换做右式

鸟戏

鸟伸

1. 两手腹前相迭，上举至头前上方，耸肩缩颈手掌水平，身体稍前倾，尾锥上翘，吸气。

2. 两手下按至腹前，再向后呈人字形分开后伸，

3. 重心右移后，左腿向后伸，做燕子飞行状。

4. 两膝伸直保持身体稳定。还原姿势。

鸟飞

1. 手心向上，两手指尖在腹前相对，膝部弯曲，重心移向右脚。

2. 两臂展开，做鸟飞起状，左腿提起，右脚慢慢伸直，展开的双手比肩略高，

3. 右脚下蹲，双手下按在腹前相对，左脚尖点地。

4. 两臂再次展开飞起，双手高举至头顶，手背相对，右脚慢慢伸直，左腿随着身体提高。

5. 右脚下蹲，双手下按在腹前相对，重心换到左脚，重复以上动作。

6. 手臂飞起时吸气，下落时呼气。

第九册生字表（简体体/部首/繁体）

第一课			第二课			第三课			第四课			第五课			第六课		
筑	竹	築	伙	人	伙	初	示	初	顾	页	顧	诵	言	誦	宿	宀	宿
薪	艹	薪	伴	人	伴	引	弓	引	咸	戈	鹹	限	阜	限	舍	人	舍
杂	木	雜	敞	攴	敞	庭	广	庭	陈	阜	陳	冠	冖	冠	遗	辶	遺
寓	宀	寓	厅	厂	廳	竟	音	竟	椒	木	椒	志	士	志	控	手	控
租	禾	租	证	言	證	尿	尸	尿	胡	月	胡	否	口	否	确	石	確
舱	舟	艙	检	木	檢	炎	火	炎	采	采	采	荒	艹	荒	躁	足	躁
甚	一	甚	签	竹	簽	喷	口	噴	烈	火	烈	凉	冫	涼	剔	刀	剔
贸	贝	貿	托	手	托	鼻	鼻	鼻	叔	又	叔	悔	心	悔	泼	水	潑
术	木	術	沈	水	沈	涕	水	涕	醋	酉	醋	沮	水	沮	羞	羊	羞
婆	女	婆	输	车	輸	染	木	染	祭	示	祭	丧	十	喪	幽	山	幽
销	金	銷	套	大	套	严	一	嚴	恭	心	恭	绪	糸	緒	焦	火	焦
制	刀	制	顿	页	頓	脾	月	脾	源	水	源	散	攴	散	愤	心	憤
虑	虍	慮	腔	肉	腔	珍	王	珍	守	宀	守	悲	非	悲	怒	心	怒
扬	手	揚	忱	心	忱	益	皿	益	辈	非	輩	佳	人	佳	疑	匕	疑
勤	力	勤	朗	月	朗	募	艹	募	盐	皿	鹽	衬	衣	襯	察	宀	察
浓	水	濃	聊	耳	聊	帐	巾	帳	堡	土	堡	寂	宀	寂	析	木	析
厚	厂	厚	祸	示	禍	操	手	操	攻	工	攻	寞	宀	寞	乱	舌	亂
优	人	優	延	廴	延	防	阜	防	渡	水	渡	暂	日	暫	荣	木	榮
缺	缶	缺	误	言	誤	慰	心	慰	据	手	據	淡	水	淡	竞	立	競
列	歹	列	承	一	承	抗	手	抗	谱	言	譜	弦	弓	弦	诚	言	誠
择	手	擇	委	禾	委	贡	工	貢	孙	子	孫	序	广	序	训	言	訓
填	土	填	辩	辛	辯	献	犬	獻	忠	心	忠	悠	心	悠	权	木	權
绩	糸	績	武	止	武	依	人	依	编	糸	編	若	艹	若	损	手	損
泪	水	淚	喊	口	喊	项	工	項	婚	女	婚	帝	巾	帝	失	丿	失